KU-515-501

TOWARDS POST-MODERNISM

COLLINS, MICHAEL
TOWARDS POST-MODERNISM. DESIGN
SINCE 1851. MICHAEL COLLINS.
745.4441   38-727282

OR 6/93

30130504177532

COLLEGE LIBRARY
COLLEGE OF TECHNOLOGY
CARNARVON ROAD
SOUTHEND-ON-SEA, ESSEX

TOWARDS POST-MODERNISM
DESIGN SINCE 1851 · MICHAEL COLLINS

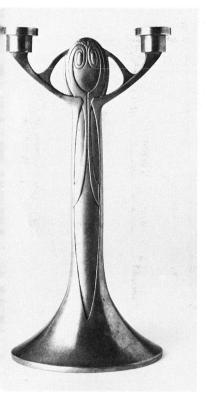

Published for the Trustees of the British Museum
by British Museum Publications

745.4441 COL

© 1987 The Trustees of the British Museum
Published by British Museum Publications Ltd
46 Bloomsbury Street, London WC1B 3QQ

British Library Cataloguing in Publication Data

Collins, Michael
   Towards post-modernism: design since 1851.
   1. Design—History—19th century
   2. Design—History—20th century
   I. Title   II. British Museum. *Trustees*
   745.4'441   NK1175

ISBN 0-7141-0548-1

ESSEX COUNTY LIBRARY

Designed by Harry Green

Set in Ehrhardt
and printed in Great Britain
by BAS Printers Limited, Over Wallop, Hampshire

FRONT COVER Silver tea and coffee service in a pedimented
case, designed by Aldo Rossi for Alessi, 1981.
(Photo: Alessi)

X FV 82930

745.4441.

CONTENTS

To Liz Wright, painter, and Lemmy, her dog

'I think of the postmodern attitude as that of a man who loves a very cultivated woman and knows he cannot say to her "I love you madly" because he knows that she knows (and that she knows that he knows) that these words have already been written by Barbara Cartland. Still there is a solution. He can say, "As Barbara Cartland would put it, I love you madly."'

UMBERTO ECO, quoted by Charles Jencks

ACKNOWLEDGEMENTS

I should like to thank first and foremost Neil Stratford, Keeper of the Department of Medieval and Later Antiquities at the British Museum, for his enthusiasm at all times and his constant support for the Museum's Modern Collection, which I assembled within his Department from 1979. My appreciation also goes to Professor David Bindman of Westfield College, University of London, for his excellent teaching, and to his wife, Frances Carey, for her advice as a colleague; also to friends abroad, especially Dr Rüdiger Joppien and Dr Carl Wolfgang Schumann for furthering my interest in German design as well as German wine. Dr Joppien kindly read the manuscript and commented on it.

At British Museum Publications my warmest thanks go to Celia Clear and to Teresa Francis, who has been attentive and encouraging throughout the preparation of this book.

In addition to those who very generously provided photographs and whose names will be found in the Photographic Acknowledgements, I wish to express my sincere thanks to Catherine McDermott of Kingston Polytechnic, Nicola Redway of Sotheby's, Andrew Higgott of the Architectural Association, Roger Sykes of Chelsea School of Art, Sam Fogg, Judy Rudoe of the Department of Medieval and Later Antiquities, British Museum, Andy Tilbrook and Michael Whiteway.

Finally, I should like to thank all my friends and students at West Surrey College of Art and Design for tolerating so many conversations about Post-Modernism with the required sense of humour.

MICHAEL COLLINS
London 1987

INTRODUCTION

This book on design covers the 'modern' age and its evolution towards Post-Modernism. For our purposes, the concept 'modern' has developed from nineteenth-century French literature and art. Honoré de Balzac, and after him Charles Baudelaire, claimed that beauty existed in modernity, in *la vie moderne*. In painting, this led to an admiration for Courbet, Realism and Impressionism. In architecture, iron was the quintessentially 'modern' material, and it became impossible to ignore its implications: the neo-classical architect Karl Friedrich Schinkel and the Gothic revival architect Eugène Viollet-le-Duc both admired it; the former's sketchbook from his British tour in 1826 is full of references to its use. Yet in the influential English critic John Ruskin it provoked a hatred and a spirit of anti-modernity; he loathed the 1851 Crystal Palace and resigned in protest at the use of iron for the Oxford Museum of 1855–60, a project with which he had himself been associated.

But Ruskin's attitude was far from typical, and the seeds of modernity had been thoroughly sown. Emile Zola's follower Joris Karl Huysmans wrote in his *En Ménage* of 1881: 'Oh, what insufferable bores they are, the people who sing the praises of the apse of Notre-Dame and the rood-screen at St Etienne-du-Mont! . . . very well, but what about the Gare du Nord and the new Hippodrome?' And Zola himself wrote in *L'Oeuvre* (1886): 'Dubuche . . . turned over to building . . . they were the old theories he had picked up from the revolutionary friends of his youth . . . he went in for tiling and terra-cotta decorations, vast constructions of glass and iron, especially iron – iron beams, iron staircases, iron roofs'. Zola was writing only a year before the construction of the Eiffel Tower, the prophetic icon of the Modern movement.

Since that time, a determinist, Whig and progressive view of visual history has been dominant, reaching its peak in the International Modern period of the 1920s and 1930s and extending into the 1960s. Post-totalitarian, post-holocaust, post-Modernist thought has attempted to break that mould and to search for evolution rather than revolution, wit and humour rather than earnest social engineering, and individuality rather than collectivism. Post-Modernism takes stock of the old as well as absorbing the shock of the new.

Exactly a century after Zola's *L'Oeuvre* we stand at a point where it may be avant-garde to be rear-guard. We are searching for a design vocabulary which extends beyond basic language and basic structure. This development of design language has reached a most exciting point now in the 1980s. After a century of 'modernity', the desire for less has been replaced by a need for more. This book surveys the evolutionary as well as revolutionary aspects of design history for the student and general reader.

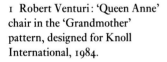

1 Robert Venturi: 'Queen Anne' chair in the 'Grandmother' pattern, designed for Knoll International, 1984.

1 ORNAMENT ON EVERYTHING
THE NINETEENTH-CENTURY ECLECTICS

In 1966, the American architect Robert Venturi made an appeal for 'complexity and contradiction' in architecture, with 'elements that are hybrid rather than pure', and these same words that sum up the aims of Post-Modernist design in the 1970s and 1980s might equally well be used to define the art and design of the period 1851 to 1914.

In analysing this period, we are faced with many separate, often interwoven, issues, including the battle of the styles, the question of the 'morality' of manufacturing industry and its outpourings, and problems related to materials, colour and symbolism. It is sufficient for the purposes of this analysis to accept that the characteristic style of late eighteenth-century architecture was neo-classicism, with only an undercurrent of 'Gothick'. The architecture of the British Museum by Sir Robert Smirke (1823) is a perfect example of the neo-Greek classicism prevailing at the beginning of the nineteenth century; another, earlier, example is Sir John Soane's house in Lincoln's Inn Fields (1813).

If, however, we look at the architecture of John Nash, we can observe that although his work, especially in Regent's Park, London, between 1810 and 1825, is essentially classical, he was also capable of designing in the 'castle Gothic' style, for example at Caerhays Castle, Cornwall (1808), and in the 'Hindu' style, at the famous Royal Pavilion in Brighton (1815–23). Nash's eclecticism sets a pattern for architecture which is repeated many times in the decorative arts throughout the nineteenth century. Quite logically, architects were also the leading designers of the age, because new buildings require furniture and furnishings. Meanwhile, large factories, such as Josiah Wedgwood's pottery in Staffordshire, continued to produce ceramics mainly in the fashionable neo-classical taste. In the first quarter of the nineteenth century, Gothic and neo-classical existed quite happily side by side and as alternative styles, just as Chinese and Gothic had done in Thomas Chippendale's eighteenth-century furniture.

The burning down of the old Houses of Parliament in 1834 was perhaps more than any other the event that heralded the Victorian style wars, for the competition to replace them specified designs in the Gothic or Tudor manner. A 'classicist' won the competition, aided by a Gothic detailer and draughtsman. They were, respectively, Sir Charles Barry and Augustus Welby Pugin, and although the latter complained that the Houses of Parliament were 'All Grecian, Sir; Tudor details on a classic body', it was Pugin's Gothic style which was to have the most influence on design before the Great Exhibition of 1851. Pugin's father had helped John Nash with his Gothic detailing, and his son took a precocious interest in drawing: at the age of

2 A. W. N. Pugin: Silver-gilt ciborium made by Hardman for St Mary's Church, Clapham, London, 1851.

fifteen he was seen copying a Dürer drawing in the British Museum Print Room by a member of the firm of silversmiths Rundell & Bridge and asked to design metalwork for them. At the same time, his father asked him to design furniture in the Gothic style for George IV at Windsor Castle.

Pugin was not slow to recognise the historical relationship between Gothic forms and the pre-Reformation Church, and in 1835, a year before publishing his polemical and vituperative *Contrasts*, he converted to Roman Catholicism. *Contrasts* is a vitriolic satire on neo-classicism; broadly, Pugin sees neo-classical architecture as a blot on the landscape, and argues that, as the Greeks were pagans, an imitation of their style is theologically inappropriate to church building. He turned the aesthetic argument for Gothic into a crusade, a battle to be won for Christianity. His conversion to Catholicism was an extreme move in this regard, even if the Oxford Movement, begun at that university by Keble, Newman and Pusey in 1833 with the aim of restoring High Church ideals within the Church of England, was leading in a similar direction.

Pugin's crusade against neo-classicism in favour of the Gothic revival fed the flames of the debate about what style was appropriate for church architecture. His next book, *The True Principles of Pointed or Christian Architecture* (1841), stated: 'It is essential to ecclesiastical propriety that the ornaments introduced about churches should be appropriate and significant.'

3 A. W. N. Pugin: Ceramic bread plate for Minton, about 1850.

This search for 'appropriate and significant' ornament became a 'holy grail' for Pugin and resulted, for example, in his designs for church tiles executed by Minton and his famous bread plate by the same firm. In common with the rest of his generation, Pugin was prepared to use industrial processes for the good of the Church, but he remained thoroughly inventive. Another architect, William Butterfield, objected on 'archaeological' grounds to Pugin's use of blue in tiles, as it was not a colour that 'existed' in the Middle Ages. Pugin's retort was that if medieval craftsmen had had the colour, they would have used it. Here the 'morality' of the archaeologist conflicted with Pugin's more modern approach. His bread plate, made about 1850, includes many codes and symbols. The newness of its colour makes it striking and arresting; the slogan it bears – 'waste not want not' – is moralising and must refer to recent contemporary events of the 'hungry forties' decade, such as the repeal of the Corn Laws in 1846 and the famine in Ireland; and the centre bears a stylised design of wheatsheaves, thus suiting decoration to function.

Pugin's interest in the relationship between decoration and function is echoed by the work of Summerly's Art Manufactures, a group of painters and sculptors, none of whom had any professional design

training. Their leader, Sir Henry Cole, was a talented civil servant who became the first director of the South Kensington Museum (later the Victoria & Albert). Cole had studied under the watercolourist David Cox, and in the 1840s he became involved in the production of books with other artists. In 1845 the Society of Arts held a competition to promote design, and Cole won, using the pseudonym Felix Summerly. When designing his prize-winning tea-set, he went to the British Museum to consult 'Greek earthenware for authority on handles'. The styles used by the Summerly group were mainly classical and rococo, and they paid great attention to suiting ornament to the purpose of the object. Thus the painter Richard Redgrave designed classical water carafes and jugs with water-plant decoration enamelled on the glass; and the sculptor John Bell's rococo revival fish-servers were given blades in the shape of a fish and Parian handles depicting a fisher-boy. Cole and Redgrave were also joint editors of the monthly *Journal of Design and Manufacture*, which ran between

4 John Bell: Flax knife, paper knife, two bread knives and two pairs of fish-servers, with parian porcelain or ivory handles, made by Joseph Rogers & Sons for Summerly's Art Manufactures, 1847–8.

1849 and 1852 and was influential in the area of design and the applied arts.

All these developments were important factors in the run-up to the Great Exhibition of 1851, which grew out of the Society of Arts' revived concern with industrial design. The Great Exhibition was the product of many interests: Cole had naturally been appointed to the executive committee in 1849, and he brought with him the expertise of the Summerly group. He also served on the Royal Commission for the exhibition, under the chairmanship of the Prince Consort, who was particularly interested in design education. Another prominent German figure in the organisation of the exhibition was the architect Gottfried Semper, a refugee from the revolutions of 1848–9, who designed several sections. The great Pugin was asked to organise the Medieval Court and act as juror; Sir Joseph Paxton was to design the glass and iron structure of the Crystal Palace, and Owen Jones, whose work we shall meet shortly, planned the colour schemes of the interior. The whole enterprise was, as one might expect, utterly incoherent, as such world fairs were always destined to be. Indeed, critics within the exhibition and outside it were even questioning whether Britain should be industrialised at all. Paxton asked Pugin what he thought of the building and was told: 'you had better keep on building greenhouses, and I will keep to my churches and cathedrals'. John Ruskin, painter, writer, critic and anti-industrialist, did not need to be asked – again, it was a 'greenhouse larger than ever greenhouse was built before'. The 1,851-foot long building contained over eight miles of display area and some of the ugliest artefacts ever produced, by virtually every important country in the world.

The aesthetic failure of the exhibition was no great surprise. Government schools of design had been set up only as recently as 1837, and their first director was the painter William Dyce. Henry Cole, John Bell and Richard Redgrave had all been involved, but of these none, significantly, were professional designers. Redgrave concluded in his report on the exhibition that 'there could be no doubt that half the ornament in the Great Exhibition and consequently the labour expended on it, is in excess'. The Government schools did, however, produce one brilliant designer, Christopher Dresser, whose greatest work dates from the 1870s and 1880s, but at this stage it is sufficient to record that the Arts and Crafts movement was born as a result of the excesses of industrial design and in opposition to the automatic processes involved in mass manufacture.

Before discussing the Arts and Crafts movement, it is important to look more closely at nineteenth-century attitudes towards colour. The neo-classicism of the eighteenth century had relied heavily on the monochrome 'noble simplicity and calm grandeur' of Greek architecture as it was understood by the generation of the great German art-historian Johann Joachim Winckelmann. The 'discovery' that Greek architecture was in fact polychromatic, as revealed, for example, in J. I. Hittorf's *Architecture polychrome chez les Grecs* of 1830, was a shock. Equally startling were the debates about whether the Parthenon sculptures had been coloured. The nineteenth-century interest in colour coincides with the development of chromolithography, first used in books such as Hittorf's and, a few years later, Owen Jones's *Alhambra* (1836–45) and Ludwig Gruner's *Specimens of Ornamental Art* (1850). A further fillip was provided by research into colour theory published by the chemist Michel Eugène Chevreul who, from 1824, was in charge of the dyeing process at the Gobelins tapestry works in France. His *Principles of Harmony and Contrast of Colour* (1839) was a watershed for designers and artists alike, and led to an awareness of colour principles as well as to the production of synthetic aniline dyes. Chevreul's work was to influence a whole generation, including the Pre-Raphaelites.

It is in this context that the debate between Pugin and Butterfield over the use of the colour blue in tiles must be seen, and even the production of new colours, such as magenta, invented soon after the Battle of Magenta in northern Italy in 1859. At the same time, in painting, the bright colours of the Pre-Raphaelites supplanted a darker classical tradition, and Delacroix abandoned the use of black in shadows, well before Monet's total prohibition of it. Specific ideas about colour application varied from designer to designer. Owen Jones often used primaries (red, blue and yellow) on the inside of buildings, for example in the Crystal Palace, to produce a 'bloom', while his follower Christopher Dresser preferred tertiaries such as olive, citrine and russet. Even sculptors began to use colour: for example, John Gibson's famous *Tinted Venus*, begun in 1850, echoed Jones's predilection for primary colours. Gibson wrote that he 'tinted the flesh like warm ivory scarcely red, the eyes blue, the hair blonde, and the net which contains the hair golden'; and as early as 1846 he had written: 'my eyes have now become so depraved and I cannot bear to see a statue without colour'. The Victorians often preferred bright colours and revelled in their seeming originality, as Post-Modernist designers do today in a reaction against the suppression of colour in favour of white which was the hallmark of the 1930s.

Owen Jones's *Grammar of Ornament* of 1856, which was seldom out of print until the twentieth century, made the greatest contribution not only to this taste for polychromy but also to stylistic eclecticism. It was the equivalent of an encyclopedia of styles, from that of the savage tribe to the highest achievement of the arts of Islam. The book ran the gamut of the available 'language' of design styles

Plate I Owen Jones: A page from *The Grammar of Ornament*, 1856.

NINEVEH AND PERSIA. Nº1.

Plate II William Burges: Wooden cup and cover with silver mounts and enamel ornament, made for Burges's own use by Barkentin & Krall, 1878.

Plate III Louis Comfort Tiffany: Glass vase and bronze candlestick designed for his own firm, about 1900.

Plate IV *(left)* Charles Rennie Mackintosh: Wooden clock with mother of pearl and plastic face, designed for W. J. Bassett-Lowke in 1919. An example of Mackintosh's 'square' style, but also a returned compliment to his Viennese followers, such as Otto Prutscher.

Plate V Peter Behrens: Brass electric clock for AEG, about 1910. Behrens is the father of modern German product design.

Plate VI Sergei Chekhonin: Porcelain plate painted with
a Russian Revolutionary slogan, made at the Lomonossov
porcelain factory, Petrograd, about 1921. The slogan can
be translated 'There will be no end to the rule of the
workers and peasants'.

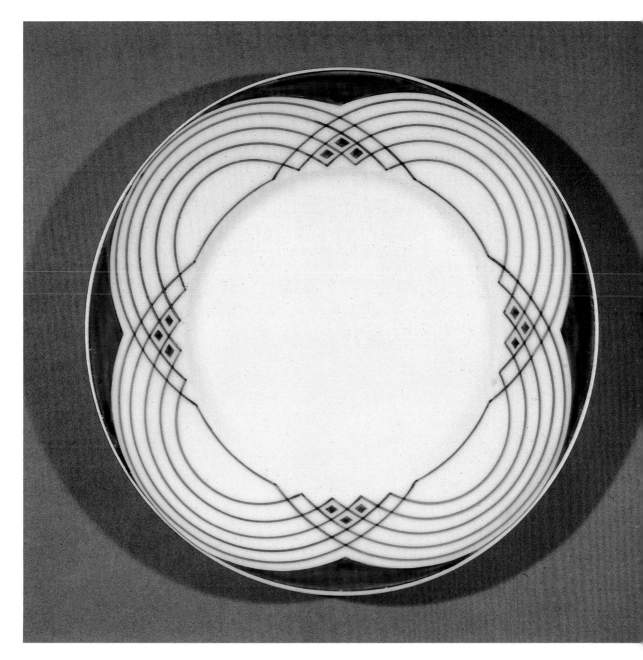

Plate VII Peter Behrens: Porcelain plate
made by Bauscher, Weiden, about 1901.

Plate VIII Alec Issigonis: 'Mini' car, 1959. 'Less is
more' on wheels. The 'Mini' also heralded the squarer
forms of the 1960s. This one is painted in Sixties
'psychedelic' colours.

5 Christopher Dresser: Ceramic cigar-tray based on a priest's bowl from Fiji, made by the Linthorpe Pottery about 1880. Dresser's use of ethnographic sources in his work was wide-ranging.

and was a testament to its author's remarkable knowledge. By the time Jones was thirty, he had travelled to Egypt, Turkey, Spain and Greece. He first showed his interest in polychromy in his lavish *Alhambra* printed with chromolithographs between 1836 and 1845 and in his designs for tiles and mosaics. The *Grammar of Ornament*, too, was a rich source of chromolithographic illustration and even contained a plate by Christopher Dresser devoted to the relatively new interest in ornament based on leaves and flowers. The language of Victorian eclecticism was codified by this book.

The *Grammar of Ornament* prompted Jones's most gifted follower, Christopher Dresser, to examine the 'morality' of past styles. Dresser trained at the Government schools of design, where he specialised in botany and had some of the best 'reforming' teachers, including Gottfried Semper, who taught design theory. Semper admired both classical and Renaissance art, but Dresser rejected the humanistic and pictorial references in the latter, probably because he felt that they had been created by painters and sculptors. He was anxious to be seen as a designer and complained that he had been trained by artists, not 'ornamentalists'. Roman and Renaissance styles were anathema to him, but even in excluding them he still had room to range through Egyptian, Greek, Islamic, Indian and Gothic 'quotations'; he also began to look towards newly appreciated cultures such as those of Peru, Mexico, Oceania and Japan. Japanese styles had become part of the European design vocabulary by the early 1860s, and Dresser shared an early interest in them with the architects Edward William Godwin and William Burges. At the same time, the influence of the Japanese print was becoming evident in the work of Manet, Monet and the other Impressionists in France. Nineteenth-century aesthetic judgements can often seem strange to us today, and Japanese art was then frequently compared with that of the Greeks. The impact of the oriental 'wave' may be difficult to understand now, but at the time its novelty was overwhelming. In 1876 Dresser went both to Japan and to America, countries whose cultures he felt had great potential for exploration. His 'world tour' was perhaps more Thomas Cook than Captain Cook, and yet he retained some of the eighteenth century's appreciation for the 'noble savage' and his art.

Since the 1930s Dresser has been principally appreciated for his scientific and 'functional' metalwork, produced by such firms as Hukin & Heath and Elkington from the late 1870s, but in fact his work has much to offer Post-Modernists. His furniture, ceramics and glass exhibit all the characteristics of 'elements which are hybrid rather than pure' and 'messy vitality over obvious unity' which were demanded by Robert Venturi in *Complexity and Contradiction in Architecture* (1966). Dresser's ceramics were based on Central and

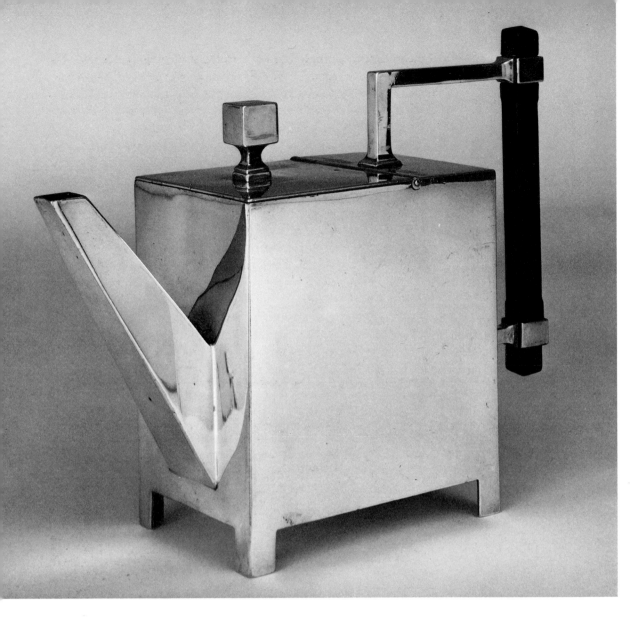

South American, Celtic, Greek, Egyptian, Islamic, Indian, Chinese and Japanese sources, and yet all were produced 'industrially' by the newest gas-kilns at the Linthorpe pottery in Yorkshire. Never slavishly archaeological, they are witty 'quotations' from many cultures. His furniture, too, mostly made by his own Art Furnishers' Alliance set up in 1880, is a mixture of several cultures. It could broadly be called 'Anglo-Japanese' in its use of ebonised wood with incised gold decoration and yet the patterning is inspired by Greek 'key' and plant forms, as well as by motifs on Moorish screens. This elision of cultures anticipates fashions of the 1980s by exactly a hundred years and to some extent echoes Chippendale's eclecticism in

6 Christopher Dresser: Electroplate teapot made by Hukin & Heath, 1878. An example of Dresser's more simple, 'functional' work.

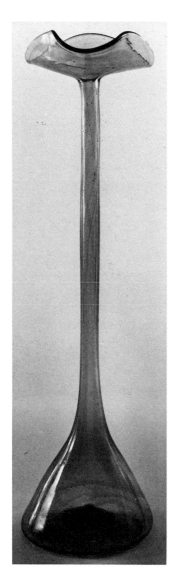

the eighteenth century. Dresser's free use of ornament shows his readiness to appreciate the past for what it could give to his own age. In the 1930s, Nikolaus Pevsner saw Dresser as a pioneer of Modern design. Today he can be seen, together with Godwin and Burges, as a pioneer of Post-Modernism.

Dresser's main occupation, however, was that of carpet and textile designer and as such he was a member of the 'flat' school, which believed that plants should be conventionalised. He stressed that

7 Christopher Dresser: Glass vase for James Couper's Clutha glassworks, Glasgow, about 1890.

designers were exactly that, and not painters, sculptors or craftsmen; he shrank from any representation of man or beast unless it was primitive or humorous. Indeed, he had a strong sense of humour, and though his interest, for example, in skeletons or cockroaches as motifs for ceramic decoration may not appeal to us today, his energetic personality embraced anti-design as well as design, 'bad form' as well as 'good', long before the similarly ambidextrous approach of Ettore Sottsass and his colleagues in Italy after the 1960s. Dresser also rejected the Renaissance tradition in his determination to see the plant as God's most important contribution to aesthetics. That is not to say that Pugin before him, and the Arts and Crafts thinkers Ruskin

8 *(above right)* Christopher Dresser: Ceramic tile for Minton, about 1880, showing Dresser's interest in Japanese design.

9 Christopher Dresser: Ebonised
chair designed for his own Art
Furnishers' Alliance, about 1883.

and Morris did not share his admiration for flower forms. The nineteenth century was, more than any other, the age of the plant, from
the anthemion on neo-classical ironwork to Hector Guimard's Art
Nouveau designs for the Paris Métro. Almost all art and design, from
Pre-Raphaelitism to Art Nouveau, may be read as a tribute to botanical forms. Indeed, apocryphally, a Victorian botanist is supposed,
on a rainy day, to have taught his students about plants in front of
Millais' painting *Ophelia*.

Like Dresser, the architect-designers E. W. Godwin and William
Burges both prefigure the eclecticism of the Post-Modern 1980s,

although they were both primarily Gothic revivalists at the beginning of their careers. Godwin was much praised by critics including Ruskin for his Gothic revival Northampton Town Hall and its furnishings (1862). At the same time, for his own home in his native Bristol he collected Japanese prints and Persian rugs. He also began to collaborate with Burges, whom he had known since the late 1850s. In 1867 they went to Ireland, where Godwin designed Dromore Castle. Some of his furniture for the castle is Gothic and some shows an interest in Turkish lattice-work, while from Chinese sources he used a satin in a colour known as Imperial yellow. Godwin also worked with the artist James McNeill Whistler on 'Anglo-Japanese' furniture, and indeed for too long he has been remembered only for his work in this style, which, in his own words, showed 'an economical building by mere grouping of solid and void'. At the same time he designed furniture for William Watt drawn from Egyptian, Greek, Chinese, Japanese, Old English and Jacobean sources. His later eclecticism reveals a weariness with simple Anglo-Japanese forms, and by the end of his career he had veered towards Tudor and Jacobean revivalism. Only in the 1980s has another architect, Robert Venturi, gone as far as Godwin in eclecticism, albeit in a single range of nine different chairs produced for Knoll in 1984.

Burges differed from Godwin in that he was largely unfettered by commercial considerations, having been left over £100,000 by his engineer father. He could therefore indulge in very expensive design gestures. Like Godwin, he enjoyed mixing cultural references, and called the Japanese display at the 1862 London International Exhibition 'the real medieval court of the exhibition'. In 1865 he met the Marquis of Bute, who had once been described as the 'richest baby in Britain' and who could afford to indulge Burges's lavish Gothic fantasies. Hans Hollein, the Austrian Post-Modernist architect, has called architecture 'an affair of the élite', and Burges and Bute certainly treated it as such in the 1870s, for example in the extravagant decorations at Castell Coch in Wales. Burges's work for his own apart-

10 E. W. Godwin: Drawing for a silver-gilt trowel (fig. 11), 1861.

11 E. W. Godwin: Silver-gilt ceremonial trowel designed for Northampton Town Hall, 1861. An early example of Godwin's interest in Gothic revival forms.

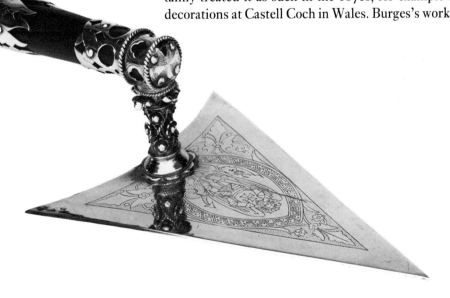

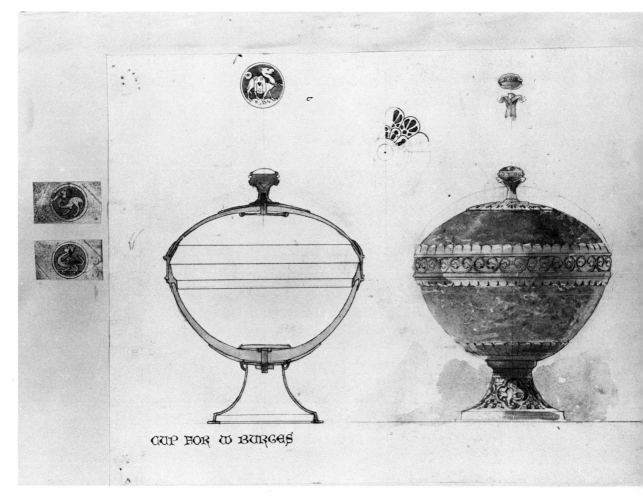

CUP FOR W BURGES

13 William Burges: Drawing for a wooden cup and cover, 1878 (see Plate II).

12 E. W. Godwin: Ebonised chair for William Watt, about 1878.

ment at Buckingham Street in London and his house in Melbury Road was eclectic, and he gave free rein to his sense of humour in designing decorative objects, such as mazers and decanters, loosely based on medieval precedents but rich in their assemblage of disparate elements, including oriental jade and Greek coins. Burges's wit even extended to displaying oriental ceramics in a Gothic cabinet of his own design.

Burges was most interested in the unique, crafted or painted object, and knew many of the Pre-Raphaelites, some of whom he employed to decorate his furniture. Dresser, Godwin and Burges were almost exclusively architect-designers, making working drawings for others to execute, sometimes by industrial processes. The Pre-Raphaelite painters, on the other hand, were quick to reject manufacturing industry and its implications. Anti-industrialism had long been an important issue. One has only to think of William Blake's metaphorical

14 William Burges: Gothic
revival overmantel containing
Chinese ceramics, made for his
own rooms at 15 Buckingham
Street, Strand, London, about
1877.

expression of his loathing for the Age of Reason in the 'dark satanic mills' of his poem 'Jerusalem' (*Milton*, 1804–8). The poet-painter John Ruskin had taken a severely anti-industrial stance in his writings, attacking the use of locomotives and machine-made ornament. He stressed that honesty and truthfulness in design and manufacture lay in making things by hand, and that making by hand was a source of joy for the craftsman. As well as criticising the Crystal Palace, he dissociated himself from the Venetian revival Oxford Museum of 1855, which he admired as a building but eventually disliked because it had an iron and glass roof.

Ruskin was not a designer and his views were sometimes unduly negative, but they struck a chord with two Oxford undergraduates, William Morris and Edward Burne-Jones, who were preparing to take holy orders. By 1855 they had abandoned their Church vocations in order to become an architect and painter respectively. The core of the Arts and Crafts movement was established in 1856 when Morris went to work in the office of the Gothic revivalist G. E. Street, where he met the architect Philip Webb. In the same year, Morris and Burne-Jones were introduced to the Pre-Raphaelite painter Dante Gabriel Rossetti.

In 1861, Morris found himself unable to purchase what he considered to be beautiful products for his newly built home, the Red

15 Philip Webb: Oak
trestle table in a robust,
stripped Gothic revival
style, designed for
Morris & Co., about 1862.

16 William Morris: 'Larkspur'
wallpaper, 1874.

17 William de Morgan: Hand-
painted ceramic tile, about 1888.

House, designed by Webb. He therefore started his own firm, Morris, Marshall, Faulkner & Co., where he employed Webb, Burne-Jones and Rossetti. At first their work, especially that of Webb, was in a robust, unadorned and 'truthful to materials' Gothic revival style, in which the bones of the construction were honestly revealed. Morris himself abandoned architecture and painting in favour of designing textiles, wallpaper, stained glass and, later, books. He is a counterpart in the decorative arts of the Pre-Raphaelites with their *horror vacui*, and he also shared their sense of the morality of hard work. His motto was 'Als Ik Kan' (as much as I can do), and indeed he may have tried to do too much. Without any professional training, he did his best to become proficient in almost all the lesser arts. If, however, he thought that he had failed at something, such as the handcrafting

18 The shop window of Morris & Co. at 449 Oxford Street, London, about 1885.

of tiles, he would encourage others to perfect it, in this case William de Morgan, who became one of the greatest craft tile-makers of the age.

Morris's company (renamed Morris & Co. in 1875) therefore had its origins in his dislike of the industrial products of the modern age. Its work was favourably received at the International Exhibition of 1862 and has influenced craftsmen ever since. Morris became a socialist, with a yearning for a return to the medieval system of guilds. Like Ruskin, he challenged industrial progress, believing that raw capitalism could be checked through the alternative of handwork. As a result, his company's products were expensive, for his workers were not wage slaves and there was no way round the problem of how to provide joy through labour at an economically viable level.

27 · ORNAMENT ON EVERYTHING

19 A. H. Mackmurdo: Cabinet for the Century Guild, about 1885.

20 W. A. S. Benson: Brass oil lamp, designed for his own firm, about 1900.

Morris's ideas spawned several craft 'guilds' which became intellectual collectives. In the 1880s the most prominent of these was Arthur Heygate Mackmurdo's Century Guild. Mackmurdo had travelled to Italy with Ruskin in 1874 and met Morris in 1877. He founded the Century Guild in 1882, and it continued until 1888. It has often been said that Mackmurdo's floral fretwork furniture and his textile designs, which are an extension of Morris's patterning, are forerunners of Art Nouveau, but much of his work is in fact classical and 'Queen Anne' in spirit. He contributed to a stylistic change in Arts and Crafts furniture by using rich woods such as mahogany, characteristic of the eighteenth century. This ran counter to the general belief among Arts and Crafts designers that English oak was the most appropriate material. Even Morris's firm practised a form of eighteenth-century revivalism from the 1880s, especially the younger architects George Jack and William Benson. Jack, an excellent wood-

21 W. A. S. Benson: Mahogany and satinwood buffet, for Morris & Co., about 1890.

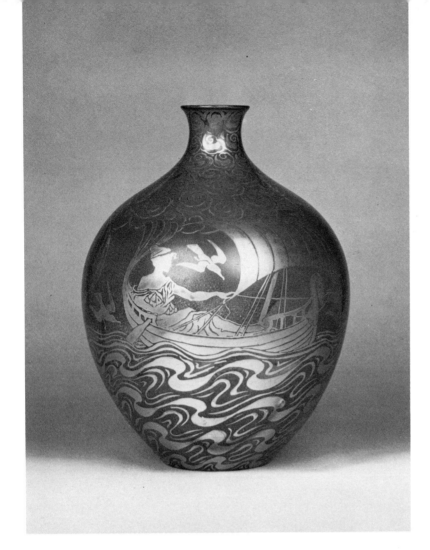

22 Walter Crane: Ceramic vase
for Pilkington's Royal
Lancastrian pottery, about 1906,
combining Arts and Crafts design
with Greek and Japanese sources.

carver, designed inlaid furniture, often in mahogany. Benson was primarily a metalworker, but he also designed furniture, much of it in mahogany inlaid with satinwood and sometimes with marble tops. Interiors by Benson often contain 'Georgian' furniture of simple elegance, and from the late 1880s Morris & Co. even began to include what we would today call 'reproduction' Georgian furniture in its catalogues. The Arts and Crafts movement has often been labelled as the expression of a simple design language, but its products of the 1880s, when the plainer Gothic forms of Philip Webb were replaced by complex references to the eighteenth century, have considerable interest for the Post-Modernists of today.

Many late Arts and Crafts designers demonstrated a similar eclecticism. The painter and illustrator Walter Crane adopted fashionable 'Queen Anne' and 'Japanese' styles for his books and tiles, and yet the influence of neo-classicism can still be seen in his work, particu-

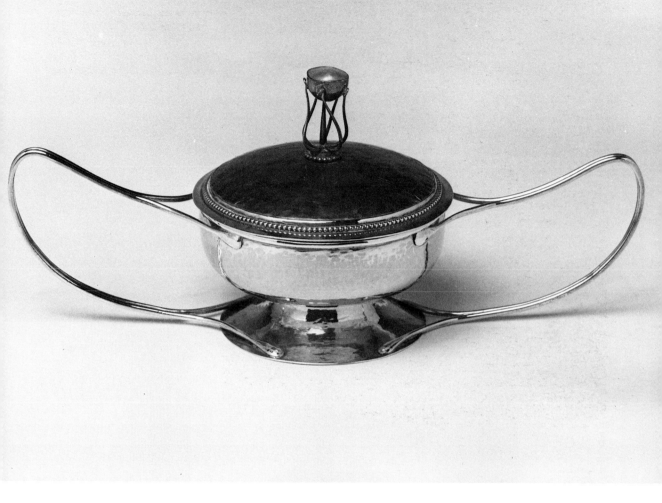

23 C. R. Ashbee: Silver and enamel cup and cover, designed for his own Guild of Handicraft, 1902.

larly in his rendering of drapery, which owes much to the survival of the style in the academic painting of Lord Leighton or Sir Lawrence Alma-Tadema. Crane often compared Japanese art to that of the Greeks, and his own work frequently combined Japanese and classical elements with a fondness for swirling lines that is culled from Morris and yet looks forward to Art Nouveau. His work was much admired and exhibited in Europe, where it was seminal for the asymmetrical, curvilinear Art Nouveau style, although Crane himself was disparaging about this Continental child of the late Arts and Crafts.

Crane had been a founder-member of the Art Workers' Guild, to which the metalworker and designer Charles Robert Ashbee was elected in 1897. Ashbee had already started his own Guild of Handicraft in 1888, inspired by his meeting with Morris a year earlier. He worked mainly in metal, hammered by hand, enamelled or embellished with a cabochon stone, and these are general characteristics of Arts and

Crafts metalwork. The sinuous, attenuated lines of Ashbee's designs also contributed to the birth of the far more curvilinear Art Nouveau style.

Ashbee was a great admirer of American Arts and Crafts developments, which ran parallel to those in Britain, and in 1900 he visited the American architect Frank Lloyd Wright. Despite long-standing connections with French Beaux-Arts training, America had many important Anglophile designers, and English influences were beginning to make themselves felt. An English-born pupil of Owen Jones, Jacob Wrey Mould, settled in New York in 1852, after assisting Jones with the polychrome decoration of the Crystal Palace and with his chromolithographic books. Mould's All Saints Church in New York (1855) introduced polychromy to the United States. William Burges also produced work for America, where his Trinity College, Hartford (Conn.), was begun in 1873. At about the same time, the Philadelphia architect Frank Furness began to adopt conventionalised plant ornament, largely based on the work of Dresser. Furness is best remembered for having employed Louis Sullivan in 1873, before the latter departed for Chicago: Sullivan eventually became the mentor of Frank Lloyd Wright. All three architects were interested in ornament, although their principal contribution was the development of the high-rise building, especially in Chicago. Only Sullivan could have

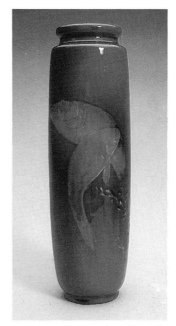

25 Albert R. Valentien: Ceramic vase made by the Rookwood Pottery, Cincinnati, Ohio, 1894 – a characteristic product of American interest in the Japanese decorative arts.

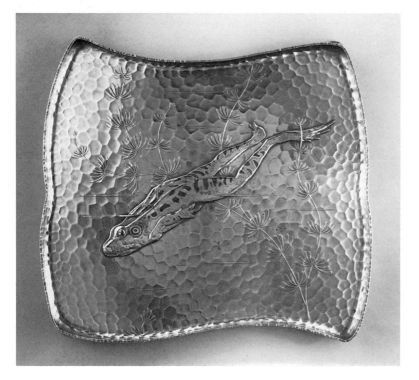

24 Tiffany & Co.: Silver tray, about 1880, strongly influenced by Japanese design and metalworking techniques.

26 Artus van Briggle: Ceramic vase made at the Van Briggle Pottery, Colorado Springs, Colorado, 1902.

written in Chicago in 1896 an article entitled 'Loftiness is to the artist-nature its thrilling aspect'. In the same article Sullivan made the famous statement 'Form ever follows function. This is the law', which became a catchphrase in design circles right up to the 1960s. What distinguished American architecture was its optimism that a truly American style might be achieved. This idea had already been expressed, for example, in Walt Whitman's lines, 'Here first the duties of today . . . / . . . the towering roofs, the lamps, / the solid-planted spires tall shooting to the stars' ('The United States to Old World Critics', 1876).

American decorative arts followed in the wake of British developments. 'Art' furniture was produced, in the so-called 'Eastlake' style, after Charles Eastlake's *Hints on Household Taste*, first published in England in 1868. The Glasgow-born decorator Daniel Cottier sold Anglo-Japanese furniture in America, and Kimble and Cabus produced highly eclectic furniture for the Philadelphia Centennial Exhibition of 1876 which drew strongly on the work of Christopher Dresser and his pupil John Moyr Smith. Dresser had visited Philadelphia in 1876, and then Chicago, where he was favourably impressed by American furniture. In New York, he had been commissioned by the silversmiths Tiffany & Co. to collect Japanese objects for them, and did so extensively during his visit to Japan in 1876. Edward C. Moore, Tiffany's principal designer, collected oriental ceramics (which he eventually left to the Metropolitan Museum of Art) and the designs executed under his leadership, quite possibly by Japanese craftsmen, show a thorough understanding of oriental metalworking techniques.

Moore's orientalism influenced the young Louis Comfort Tiffany, painter, stained glass designer and glass-maker. Tiffany's sinuous, organic glass will be examined in more detail in the next chapter, but it is important to stress here that the Art Nouveau elements in his work have their origins in 1880s eclecticism, and that, like Edward Moore, Tiffany was inspired by the arts of both Japan and Islam.

America also rapidly copied European interest in 'art pottery', producing excellent work such as that of the Rookwood Pottery in Cincinnati or of Artus Van Briggle in Colorado Springs. The success of 'art pottery' was the result of a growing awareness of the minor arts as well as the ubiquitous late nineteenth-century desire for artistic possessions in the home. Oriental glazing effects are a hallmark of this 'art pottery' just as copper and brass are of Arts and Crafts work. American standards of production were very high, sometimes closer to French than English work in quality of 'finish'; indeed, Continental work in the Art Nouveau style came to inspire designers in the United States. In this context it is interesting to note that Russian silver manufacturers, who had excellent standards – among them Pavel Ovtchinnikov – produced work for Tiffany & Co. in the 1880s.

Britain had taken a lead in establishing a design museum (now the Victoria & Albert) for 'the improvement of public taste in design'. Its educational role was immense, and it was imitated in other countries, especially America. One pupil of the English Government schools of design, Walter Smith, did much for design education in the United States; while another, Christopher Dresser, lectured at the newly founded Philadelphia Museum. Several American museums were also laid out according to English principles. America participated strongly in the many International Exhibitions held during the second half of the nineteenth century: Paris 1859; London 1862; Paris 1867; Vienna 1873; Philadelphia 1876; Paris 1878; Paris 1889; Chicago 1893 – this list can only hint at the international flavour of the period, when the artefacts of almost every culture became available for study.

The British Arts and Crafts movement also had close links with America. John Ruskin was a personal friend of Charles Eliot Norton, a Harvard graduate who became a lecturer in the history of art at the same university in 1874. Ruskin's aesthetic criticism was well known and appreciated in America, and was directly responsible for the style of, for example, Peter B. Wright's Venetian Gothic – or, more correctly, Ruskinian Gothic – National Academy of Design, built in New York during the Civil War. It nevertheless took some considerable time for Arts and Crafts ideas to develop fully in America. A leading exponent was the architect Frank Lloyd Wright, who had a strong admiration for Ruskin, Morris and Japanese art and design, and who was a founder-member of the Chicago Arts and Crafts Society in 1897. Wright used typically Arts and Crafts materials in his oak furniture and copper ornaments of the 1890s. He furnished his innovative low Prairie Houses in this style, sometimes complaining that his furniture would be replaced: 'the old furniture they possessed usually went in with the clients . . . dragging the horrors of the Old Order after them'.

Wright was, however, scathing about other American Arts and Crafts furniture, such as that produced by Gustav Stickley and by Elbert Hubbard's Roycroft group. Stickley, who was inspired by the work of Charles Voysey in England, began to exhibit Arts and Crafts furniture in 1900, and published an influential magazine, the *Craftsman*, which ran from the turn of the century to the First World War. Hubbard was also influenced by British design, especially that of Morris, and produced books, furniture and leatherwork. The architects and interior designers Charles Sumner Greene and his brother

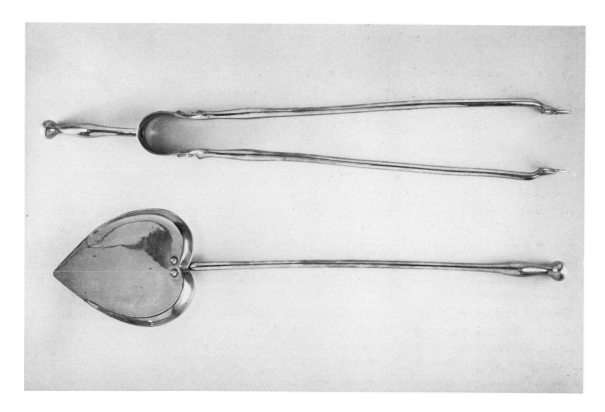

28 C. F. A. Voysey: Brass coal shovel and fire tongs, made by Thomas Elsley, about 1900.

27 Frank Lloyd Wright: Copper weed-holder, made by James A. Miller & Brother, Chicago, about 1893. American Arts and Crafts design at its best.

Henry Mather Greene also worked in the Arts and Crafts style after settling in California in the early 1890s. Their architecture is of interest in its frequent use of timber, and their source of inspiration is sometimes as Japanese as Wright's. They also produced Arts and Crafts furniture.

In the 1890s much American furniture was influenced by the work of the British designer Charles F. A. Voysey, and it is to him that we must turn in the last part of this chapter. Voysey was trained as an architect, and was much inspired by the swirling lines in the decorative patterns of Morris and of Mackmurdo, who was a friend of his. Voysey's low, roughcast, gabled architecture is almost the epitome of the Arts and Crafts style, but it was to his fabric and wallpaper designs that he owed his reputation. From 1893, his work was extensively published in the *Studio* magazine, which became the mouthpiece for British Arts and Crafts endeavours. Many of the idioms of Arts and Crafts are Voysey's innovations, such as the heart shape or tulip end seen especially on his oak pieces and his copper or brass door furniture. Voysey saw himself as the inheritor of the Gothic tradition, via Pugin, and avoided becoming a mere imitator of Morris by using more muted colours and even more rhythmic patterns.

However, Voysey came to feel his work had been misinterpreted, for he witnessed the birth of Art Nouveau – which was often attributed to him – with horror, and disowned it. In the 1930s others saw him as a pioneer of the Modern style, and he had to suffer this ignominy until his death during the Second World War. Voysey was not a Modern designer, and his individuality and xenophobia militated against his becoming involved in foreign movements. He spent his under-employed years in the 1920s designing Gothic revival furniture, heraldic stained glass and bookplates, which hardly suggest radical modernity. In only one thing was he really forward-looking, and this he shared with Frank Lloyd Wright: both men felt that the machine did have a place in the Arts and Crafts movement. The mood of 1900 was different from that of 1860, and insufficient distinction has often been made between mid-Victorian and Edwardian Arts and Crafts attitudes. In 1901, in his famous lecture in Chicago on the 'Art and Craft of the Machine', Wright stated that in the case of furniture,

29 C. F. A. Voysey: Oak chair with rush seat, 1898. The cut-out heart motif is characteristic of Voysey's work.

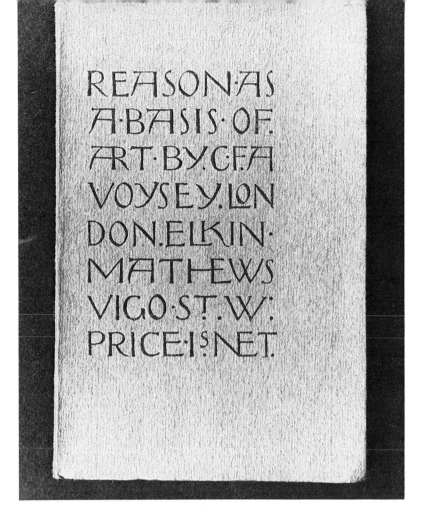

30 C. F. A. Voysey: Lettering
for a booklet entitled *Reason as a
basis of Art*, 1906.

for example, 'machines have undoubtedly placed within reach of the
designer a technique enabling him to realise the true nature of wood
in his designs harmoniously with man's sense of beauty, satisfying
his material needs with such economy as to put this beauty of wood
in use within the reach of everyone'.

The coherence of design within Wright's own work, together with
his acceptance of the machine, leads quite naturally to issues which
will be discussed in the third chapter of this book. Meanwhile it is
important to record that Arts and Crafts ornament was the precursor
of Art Nouveau, whereas Arts and Crafts furniture led, directly in
a few instances, to the Modern movement of the 1920s. As yet, Post-
Modernism in the 1980s has mainly looked back to the neo-classicism
of the eighteenth century and it can still no doubt learn much from
the nineteenth. The eclecticism of the generation of Dresser, Godwin
and Burges suggests a multicultural approach rather than a single-
minded, determinist one. There is therefore much to be gleaned from
this period when Britain still led the way in architecture and design.

2 THE WHIPLASH
ART NOUVEAU

Art Nouveau may be seen to have evolved from many of the styles outlined in the preceding chapter. Its origins lie in the British Arts and Crafts movement with its emphasis on the decorative, and the *horror vacui* of Morris's textiles and wallpapers and the restless curves of Mackmurdo's work both contributed to it. The publication of the *Studio* magazine, which first appeared in 1893, did much to make British art and design known in Europe and America. It was read widely, and even reached the café frequented by the young Pablo Picasso in Barcelona. At the same time, the Pre-Raphaelite-inspired style of Aubrey Beardsley became well known through the *Yellow Book* and other magazines. However, despite its evolution from British sources, Art Nouveau was to be quintessentially Continental, and, in being so, it was to display an ease and flair, without moral questioning, which was absent from its Arts and Crafts counterpart in the British Isles. As a decorative style it reigned supreme in the *fin-de-siècle* years from about 1890 to the outbreak of the First World War in 1914. Art Nouveau is broadly characterised by its expensive treatment of materials, attention to detail and craftsmanship, and a love of asymmetry and the sinuous curved line. The style also invaded the graphic arts, painting and sculpture, and artists such as Auguste Rodin, Constantin Meunier and Henri de Toulouse-Lautrec all produced work which can be described as Art Nouveau because of its serpentine flow.

The name Art Nouveau was never translated into English, and elsewhere the style was given many other descriptive titles. In Italy it was called *stile Liberty* after the shop founded in London by Sir Arthur Lasenby Liberty in 1875, and in Germany it was dubbed *Jugendstil* after the humorous magazine *Jugend*, first published in 1896. In France it was also called *style nouille* (noodle style) on account of its soft curvilinearity, and *style Guimard* or *style bouche de Métro* in tribute to the work of Hector Guimard for the Paris underground system entrances, begun in 1900. The name Art Nouveau in fact came specifically from the 'Maison de l'Art Nouveau', a shop opened in Paris

31 Georges de Feure: Ceramic vase designed for Samuel Bing's 'Maison de l'Art Nouveau', about 1900 – a typical piece of French figurative Art Nouveau.

in 1895 by Samuel Bing. Bing's career is characteristic of the entrepreneurial achievements of the time. He worked in a ceramics factory in his native Hamburg, and then travelled to Japan and China in 1875, a year before Christopher Dresser did the same. In 1877, two years after Liberty's opened in London, Bing established a shop in Paris called 'La Porte Chinoise', where he sold oriental artefacts. At Bing's one might encounter the American artist and designer Louis Comfort Tiffany or the Goncourt brothers, Edmond and Jules, who had done much in their writing, especially in the journal *L'Art du XVIIIe siècle*, published between 1859 and 1875, to revive interest in eighteenth-century art and most of all in Antoine Watteau. They were particularly interested in the rococo, and the sinuous quality of Art Nouveau owes much to a revival of that style. Their other main interest was Japonisme, and this too is an ingredient of Art Nouveau, with its emphasis on colour: many posters of the 1890s are strongly based on an awareness of Japanese line and the colouring of Japanese wood-block prints.

Bing himself contributed to the great Japanese cult by publishing *Artistic Japan* between 1888 and 1891. At the same time he was aware of American design, and in 1893 went on to report on the Chicago World Columbian Exposition for the French Government. While there he was particularly impressed by the architecture of Louis Sullivan, and on his return he published *Artistic America* (1895). In the same year he opened the famous Paris shop which gave its name to Art Nouveau, and commissioned his American friend L. C. Tiffany to make ten stained-glass windows for it. They were designed by eminent artists including Paul Sérusier, Henri de Toulouse-Lautrec, Pierre Bonnard and Edouard Vuillard. Bing also employed British painters such as Frank Brangwyn to design stained glass and murals, and showed the very best of British Arts and Crafts work by Morris, Benson, Crane and Voysey.

Although these British designers were admired in Europe, the compliment was not always returned. When Art Nouveau furniture was acquired by the Victoria & Albert Museum in 1900 after the Paris Exhibition there was an outcry; the collection included an exotic mahogany and marquetry cabinet by Louis Majorelle, inlaid with characteristic tree and lily decoration. British designers like Voysey and Crane disapproved of the Art Nouveau style, even though it had evolved from their own work; the latter called it a 'strange decorative disease', anticipating the loathing expressed by the Austrian Anglophile architect Adolf Loos. Bing's shop was in any case better known for its Continental Art Nouveau: furniture by Majorelle, the sinuous glass forms of Tiffany, softly curving jewellery by René Lalique, and the elegant work of the gifted Belgian Henri van de Velde.

32 Henri van de Velde: Gold
and tortoiseshell hair comb, made
by Theodor Müller, Weimar,
about 1902.

The 'Maison de l'Art Nouveau' was particularly admired by the
influential German writer Julius Meier-Graefe. Meier-Graefe went
to England in 1893 to meet Morris, and the following year founded
the influential German Art Nouveau magazine *Pan*. This had similar
aims to the *Studio* and included excellent graphic work by Van de
Velde and Peter Behrens. In 1899 Meier-Graefe opened his own shop
in Paris, and launched it as 'La Maison Moderne'. He had a sure
eye for Art Nouveau work, and especially admired Van de Velde,
whom he had visited in 1895 with Bing. Van de Velde designed the
shop and also the offices for his new magazine *Dekorative Kunst*,
another European equivalent of the British *Studio*.

Meier-Graefe's enthusiasm for Van de Velde is understandable,
for his work achieved a very high standard of excellence. Like Morris
in England and Peter Behrens in Germany, Van de Velde trained
as a painter. He was successful at this first profession, and became

33 Henri van de Velde: Silver cutlery made by Theodor Müller, Weimar, about 1902, and a porcelain plate made by Meissen, 1904.

a member of the Belgian Post-Impressionist group Les Vingt. However, he was also interested in design, read Ruskin and Morris, and even came to England to seek the latter out. From 1893 Van de Velde began to design Art Nouveau textiles and book covers, and in 1895 built his own house at Uccle (Brussels), which was visited with interest by Meier-Graefe and Bing. From then on he practised as an architect, inspired in part by the influence of the Belgian Art Nouveau architect Victor Horta, whose own house and workshops in Brussels, built between 1898 and 1900, were important landmarks in the restless *fin-de-siècle* style.

Van de Velde's work was admired in Germany, largely as a result of the publicity given to it by Meier-Graefe, and in 1900 he moved to Berlin, where he had already completed some design work. It was in Germany that he proved most influential, and in 1902 he was made artist-in-residence at the Court of Weimar. Here he designed some

42 · THE WHIPLASH

of the most beautiful silver ever produced in the Art Nouveau style, most of it made by the Weimar Court jeweller Theodor Müller. His designs for metal and ceramics exhibit all the characteristics of Art Nouveau, which had by this time become known in Germany as *Jugendstil*. Hallmarks of Van de Velde's style are a typical 'whiplash' pattern, as well as flowing curvilinearity and asymmetry.

His work was not, however, without its critics, among them Adolf Loos, who quipped somewhat unfairly: 'for an extra punishment put a criminal in a cell designed by Van de Velde'. Nevertheless, Van de Velde was a major intellectual force in Art Nouveau and in 1908 he was appointed director of the Weimar School of Arts and Crafts, where, as architect to the school, he had already constructed a new building from 1906. This school was the direct ancestor of the Bauhaus, and Van de Velde participated in the highly intelligent design debates of the period by joining the freshly formed Deutscher Werkbund in 1907. But he continued to believe in the concept of the artist-designer; his hostility to standardisation, and the simpler fact that, as a Belgian, he became an enemy alien upon the outbreak of the First World War in 1914, cost him his position in Weimar. It could be argued that Art Nouveau was in any case on the wane by then, but from 1900 to 1914 Van de Velde remained in many ways its most accomplished protagonist.

It is interesting that Van de Velde began his career as a painter, for so, too, did the great American glass artist Louis Comfort Tiffany. Tiffany was the son of the founder of Tiffany & Co., the New York silversmiths, and studied painting in America and Paris. In 1877 he founded the Society of American Artists with John La Farge and other painters; from this he formed a decorating firm, Louis C. Tiffany and Associated Artists, in 1878. Like Bing, Dresser and Liberty, he was interested in orientalism, and in this had been partly tutored by his father's associate Edward C. Moore. In the 1880s Tiffany began to design stained glass and in 1885 founded the Tiffany Glass Company. His delicate 'Favrile' (meaning hand-made) glass is characteristic of the Art Nouveau style – often elongated, fragile, and rich in colour and texture. Tiffany had met Bing at the 1889 Paris Exhibition, and the latter marketed his glass as well as favouring Tiffany with the important stained glass commission for his shop in 1895. In 1900 Tiffany Studios were established to produce work in bronze, which was often combined to splendid effect with the glass to make lamps; it was for the latter that Tiffany was best known, although the Studios produced many other objects, including medals.

Tiffany's art glass was widely admired, and its fragility inspired the German etcher Karl Köpping to produce thin blown glassware, which was also shown at Bing's. Köpping's work has all the delicacy

34 Karl Köpping: Glass made by Friedrich Zitzmann, Wiesbaden, about 1900. *Jugendstil* at its most delicate and fragile.

36, 37 Charles Rennie
Mackintosh: Silver cutlery *(top)*,
made by David Hislop, Glasgow,
1902, and nickel cutlery designed
for Miss Cranston's tea-rooms,
Glasgow, about 1905.

35 *(left)* Charles Rennie
Mackintosh: Oak chair for the
Argyle Street tea-rooms,
Glasgow, 1897. Mackintosh's
approach to Arts and Crafts
design was highly individual.

of the art of the etcher, but in glass; its fragility is the quintessence
of Art Nouveau. He became an editor of *Pan* magazine in 1896, and
included in it an etching of some of his flower-form glass.

Fundamental to the development of Art Nouveau was the contribution of a group of Scottish designers and architects, centred round
Charles Rennie Mackintosh. Mackintosh began his career in Glasgow
as a brilliant architectural draughtsman, learning much from English
and Scottish traditional architecture. He received encouragement
from F. H. Newbery, the head of the Glasgow School of Art, and
joined forces with Herbert MacNair and the Macdonald sisters,
Margaret and Frances, to form the 'Glasgow Four'. Dubbed the
'spook school', probably on account of the eerie quality in the work
of the two women, the Glasgow Four combined late Pre-Raphaelite
inspiration in graphics with an architectural sense in furniture design,
particularly that of Mackintosh, that is Arts and Crafts based. Mackintosh's work was much publicised in the *Studio* magazine in 1897 and
he was soon commissioned by a Miss Cranston to design and furnish
the tea-rooms which she was establishing in Glasgow as part of a campaign against drunkenness. As an architect, Mackintosh's sense of
space was extraordinary even for his generation. This extended even
to his designs for cutlery and candlesticks, which are, at their best,
elongated and mannered to the point where they might be described
as theatrical.

Mackintosh's work had greater influence in Austria and Germany
than it did in England, and it is impossible to define it in terms of
anything except singular invention and a unique interplay of colour
and texture. His ironwork, especially on the Glasgow School of Art
building which he designed in 1897, comes close to an abstract version
of 'botanical' Art Nouveau, and yet it was his use of rectilinear architectural forms which most inspired the Austrian designers of the day.
He designed the Scottish display at the 1900 Vienna Secession Exhibition, and in 1901 the Secession magazine, *Ver Sacrum*, praised his
work.

One of Austria's most prominent architects, Josef Hoffmann, who
in 1903 founded the Wiener Werkstätte, a Viennese Arts and Crafts
workshop, visited Mackintosh in Scotland and was influenced by him
towards adopting a rectilinear style in his own work. Indeed, he was
nicknamed '*quadratl*' Hoffmann as a result. It can be argued that Hoffmann also came to admire geometric forms during a journey to Italy
in 1895 when, repeating Schinkel's similar travels and enthusiasm of
1804, he too was impressed by plain cubic Italian farmhouses. Hoffmann's Palais Stoclet in Brussels of 1905–11 is the best example of
this phase of his career.

Financial backing for the Wierner Werkstätte was provided by Fritz

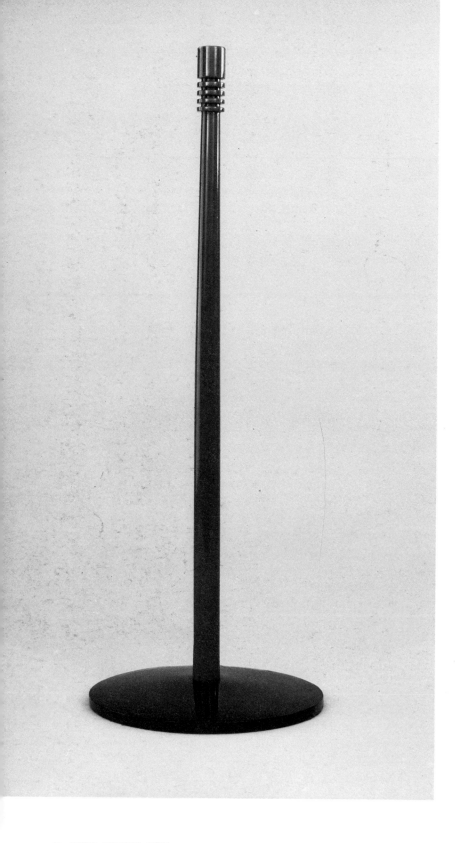

38 *(left)* Charles Rennie Mackintosh: Plastic candlestick, about 1917. An adventurous use of a relatively new material.

39 Charles Rennie Mackintosh: Silver and ebonised wood candlesticks, made by David Hislop, Glasgow, 1904.

47 · THE WHIPLASH

Wärndorfer, an Anglophile who had been inspired by C. R. Ashbee's Guild of Handicraft to form a Viennese counterpart. Besides Hoffmann, the Werkstätte's artists included Koloman Moser and Otto Prutscher. Their best work cannot be called Art Nouveau: it is square or geometric in form, in tribute to Mackintosh, in the same way that Mackintosh's late clock for his English patron W. J. Bassett-Lowke returns the compliment to the square style of his own Austrian followers. Mackintosh helped to cause the downfall of Art Nouveau simply by using an architectural style that was too rectilinear to accommodate it.

Indeed, in 1905, Hoffmann and Moser announced in their work programme for the Werkstätte that 'our guiding principle is function, utility our first condition, and our strength must lie in good proportions and the proper treatment of material. We shall seek to decorate when it seems required but we do not feel obliged to adorn at any price.' This attitude changed, especially after the First World War when Hoffmann's designs became neo-classical or neo-rococo, and his later eclecticism stands as evidence of how a simple early style may evolve towards increased decoration. His decorative work of the 1920s has been called 'decadent'; it is certainly more in accord with Viennese *Gemütlichkeit* and cosiness than his earlier square forms. Nevertheless, the learned 'quotations' of Hoffmann's later period pro-

40 Josef Hoffmann: Silver-plated coffee set for the Wiener Werkstätte, about 1909.

41, 42 Koloman Moser: Drawing *(right)* for a ladies' writing desk and interlocking chair *(below)*, made by the Wiener Werkstätte, about 1903.

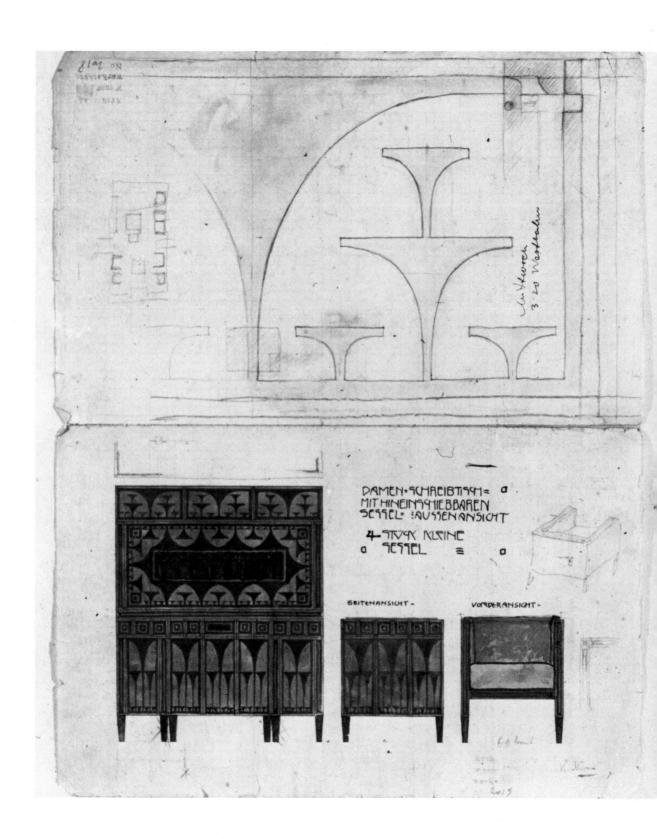

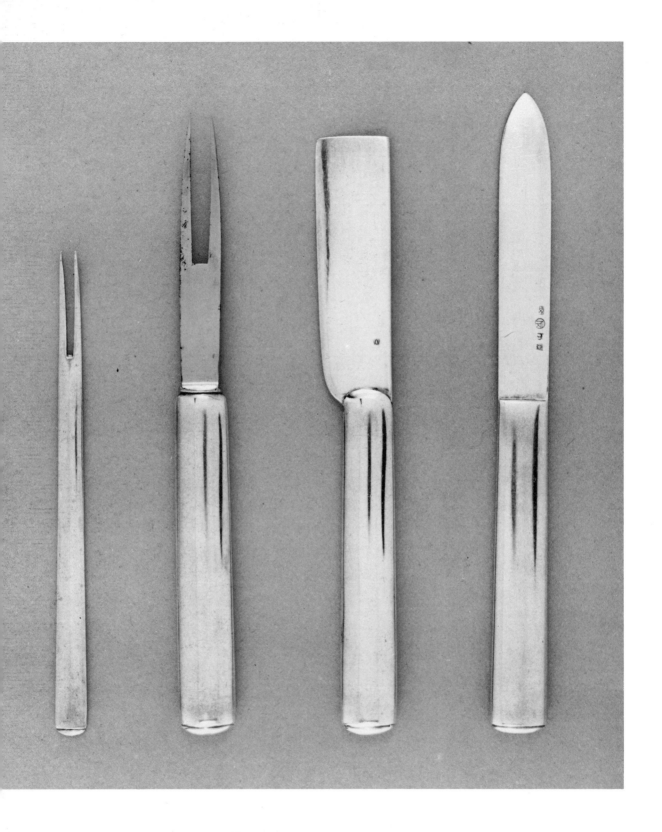

44 *(above)* Otto Prutscher:
Wine glass for E. Bakalowits und
Söhne, 1908. Prutscher's
rectilinear style is here much
inspired by the work of Charles
Rennie Mackintosh.

43 *(left)* Josef Hoffmann: Silver
cutlery made by the Wiener
Werkstätte, about 1905.

45 *(right)* Josef Hoffmann:
Silver flower basket made by the
Wiener Werkstätte, about 1905.
An example of Hoffmann's early
'square' style, influenced by
Mackintosh.

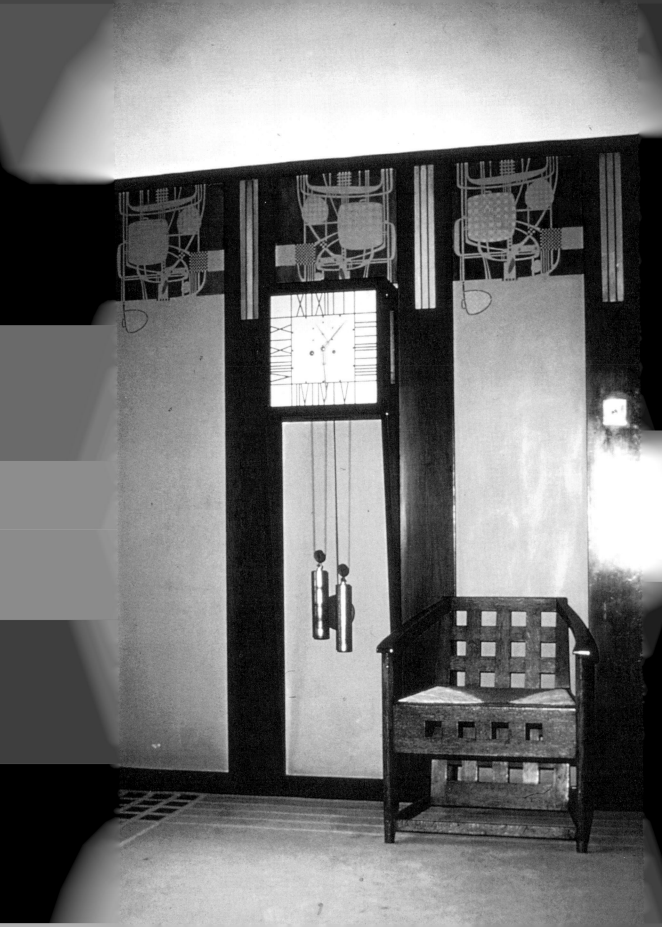

47 Josef Hoffmann: Two-handled silver cup, made by the Wiener Werkstätte, 1920.

46 Charles Rennie Mackintosh: Entrance hall, Hill House, Helensburgh, near Glasgow, 1902–3, designed for the publisher Walter Blackie.

vide Post-Modern designers with a case-history of evolution away from a simple, single-coded attitude to modernity towards a more humorous and catholic sense of ornament.

We have seen that the metalwork of Henri van de Velde was among the highest achievements of Art Nouveau. Jewellery of the period was characteristically sinuous and flowing, and another British revival made a contribution to the 'soft' style. This was the Celtic revival, most prominent in literature in the 1890s, for example in the early poems of W. B. Yeats, but also evident in the tributes to early Irish art – in particular the use of interlace in manuscripts like the Book of Kells – found in the work of Archibald Knox. Knox was a Manxman, and studied at Douglas School of Art. From 1898 he designed for Liberty, who were retailing silver and pewter in the Art Nouveau style. His work is very Celtic in inspiration, with much use

of interlace forms and a limited range of peacock blue and green enamels. His soft, sinuous shapes are probably the most typically Art Nouveau features in British design. However, Knox's objects rarely exhibit the high degree of finish of Continental work, and the same may be said for much of C. R. Ashbee's Guild of Handicraft metalwork.

Standards of exotic excellence were more readily achieved in the hands of Tiffany, Lalique or Emile Gallé. More outrageous still were the architectural fantasies of Hector Guimard, whose metal Paris Métro entrances haunt the night like vast insects from an undiscovered planet. The animal- and insect-like quality of Guimard's creations is echoed in the equally eerie structures of the aptly named

48 Josef Hoffmann: Silver cutlery made by the Wiener Werkstätte, 1923.

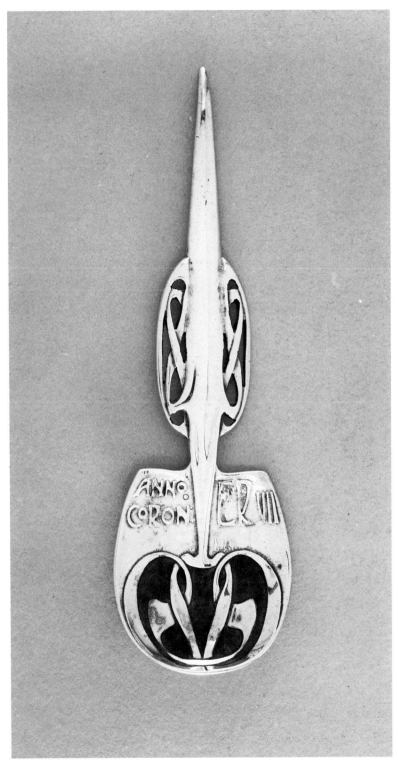

50 *(right)* Archibald Knox:
Celtic revival silver and enamel
spoon, made by Liberty for the
coronation of Edward VII, 1901.

49 Josef Hoffmann: Glass vase,
made by the Wiener Werkstätte,
about 1920. Hoffmann's later
work is often classical in
inspiration.

51 *(left)* Archibald Knox: Silver kettle and stand, made by Liberty, 1905.

52 Tiffany Studios, New York: Bronze 'Coca-Cola' medal, about 1910.

53 René Lalique: Gold and tinted horn hatpin in the form of a grasshopper, made by his own firm, about 1900.

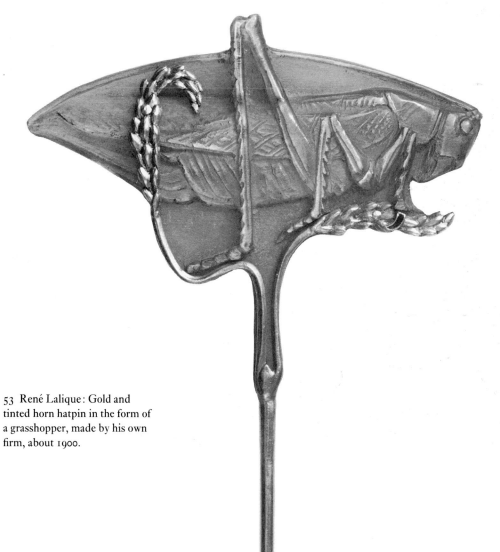

54 *(above)* Antonio Gaudí:
Dragon gate at the Güell estate,
Barcelona, 1885–8.

55 *(left)* Peter Behrens: Colour
woodcut, *Schmetterlinge auf
Seerose* (Butterflies on
Waterlilies), 1896. A *Jugendstil*
graphic design inspired by
Japanese prints.

56 *(right)* Peter Behrens: His own house in the artists' colony at Darmstadt, 1901.

57 *(below)* Hector Guimard: Doorway of the Castel Béranger, Paris, 1898. European Art Nouveau at its most extreme.

Antonio Gaudí, Spanish Gothic revivalist turned fantastical architect, whose work includes the church of the Sagrada Família and the Güell palace and park in Barcelona. Zoomorphic, biomorphic, even osteomorphic inspiration lies behind his wild, restless ironwork and furniture design, and his buildings look as though they have been sculpted from sand. In Germany, too, extreme forms of Art Nouveau or *Jugendstil* surface decoration were used by the architect E. M. A. Endell; and the graphics of Peter Behrens, such as *The Kiss*, published in the magazine *Pan*, featured a kind of 'whiplash' decoration.

59 · THE WHIPLASH

58 *(above)* Joseph Maria Olbrich: The Vienna Secession building, 1898.

59 Albin Müller: Brass and copper candlesticks, made at Darmstadt, about 1908.

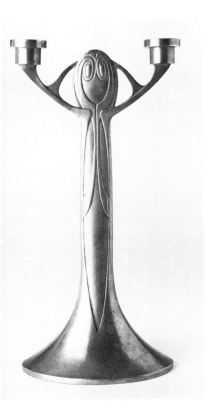

60 Joseph Maria Olbrich:
Pewter candlestick made by
Edward Hueck, Lüdenscheid,
Westphalia, about 1901.

Behrens's career underlines the problems associated with an understanding of Art Nouveau. Like many Continental designers, he
trained as a painter and became a well-known Art Nouveau graphic
artist. It was only in 1899, when he was thirty, that he began an architectural career, joining the artists' colony established at Darmstadt
by the Anglophile Grand Duke Ernst Ludwig von Hessen. Here he
met the Austrian *Jugendstil* architect and designer Joseph Maria
Olbrich, who was responsible for most of the houses in the colony.
The work of Behrens, Olbrich and Albin Müller at Darmstadt was
essentially Art Nouveau in style, but Behrens soon became interested
in Renaissance architecture: he was particularly fascinated by Floren-
tine churches with their marble-decorated façades. His architectural
break with Art Nouveau was as significant as that of Mackintosh, but
was given a further impetus by current German ideas about industrial
design and the role of the craftsman. These ideas centred round
another German Anglophile, Hermann Muthesius, who had made a
careful study of the British Arts and Crafts movement and English
domestic architecture. Muthesius was determined to push German
design towards industrialisation and he was the force behind the
foundation of the Deutscher Werkbund in 1907. In this he eventually
came into conflict with the individual, artistic temperament of Van
de Velde, who was strongly opposed to standardisation. The Werkbund had been formed to 'improve industrial products through the
combined efforts of artists, industry and craftsmen', which was in
itself a contradiction in terms. As we shall see, it continued to make
an impact in the late 1920s, but it is clear that at this time it was
Peter Behrens who best understood Muthesius's message.

Behrens had already, in 1906, been appointed designer to AEG,
the large electrical cartel based in Berlin, and in 1907 he became its
architect. His turbine factories of 1908 and his electric lamps, fans,
kettles and clocks were all part of a 'house-style' for AEG, designed
to present industrial form to a large public. His famous AEG kettles
are curious statements: industrial products which imitate Arts and
Crafts hammered surfaces but take their main inspiration from
Renaissance architectural forms. In common with a later generation
which included Ludwig Mies van der Rohe, Behrens was also
influenced by the neo-classicism of the early nineteenth-century
designer K. F. Schinkel. However, his transition from *Jugendstil* artist
to industrial designer was sometimes jerky, and his work is best seen
as the beginning of 'good form', rather than its final achievement,
which largely belonged to the Bauhaus. The German designer
Richard Riemerschmid underwent a similar evolution in his own work
and was, with Behrens, a pioneer of Werkbund forms.

The assault on Art Nouveau by industrial design and by rebellious architects contributed to its demise, but factors of cost also played an important part. Art Nouveau was a luxurious avant-garde style, available only to a few enlightened patrons. The growth of mass markets militated against its survival, even before the Great War. Even Frank Lloyd Wright, who had founded the Chicago Arts and Crafts Society in 1897 and had admired Ruskin and Morris, admitted in 1901 that the 'normal tool of civilisation' was the machine. But Wright's attitude to the machine was ambiguous. It was only a later generation which in fact took it seriously, and then from necessity, after the First World War.

Art Nouveau can thus be seen as the end of an evolution. If it developed in Europe from British Arts and Crafts work, it was also criticised as out of keeping with Anglo-Saxon restraint. One such critic, the Austrian Adolf Loos, has already been mentioned. He began attacking architectural extravagance in the late 1890s, reserving his admiration for American plumbing and simple English traditional furniture. One year after the formation of the Werkbund he published an essay, 'Ornament und Verbrechen' (Ornament and Crime), in which he indulged in a criminological survey of the effects of excess

62 Peter Behrens: Liqueur glass made by Benedikt von Poschinger, Oberzwieselau, about 1903.

61 Peter Behrens: Brass electric kettle for AEG, about 1907. The shape of the kettle owes more to Renaissance architecture than to functionalism, and the 'hammer' marks on the metal still suggest an Arts and Crafts approach.

63 Richard Riemerschmid:
Porcelain plate, made by
Meissen, 1906.

decoration. (This fear of decoration, and its association with criminality, may owe something to the writings of the Italian criminologist Cesare Lombroso, whose principal work, *L'uomo delinquente*, was published in 1889.) In his own search for a style, Loos embraced neo-classicism and Greek architecture as a form of salvation. His criticism was influential in unseating Art Nouveau: later generations agreed that a purge had been necessary and even long overdue, and perhaps today's rediscovery of ornament is only a return to the time before Art Nouveau was finally rejected.

3 FORM WITHOUT ORNAMENT
THE MODERN STYLE

We saw in the last chapter how the functionalist aesthetic of the Deutscher Werkbund emerged in contrast to the highly ornamented Art Nouveau style. After the Great War things could never be the same as they had been during the *belle époque*. Germany and Austria had been defeated and were now involved in reparations; there was economic turmoil and inflation. Conditions in the design world were ripe for change; already, during the war, in 1916, the *Deutsches Warenbuch* had depicted simple, utilitarian objects as examples of good taste. In 1924, the Werkbund published an exhibition catalogue entitled *Form ohne Ornament* (Form without Ornament), in which plain industrial design and artefacts were illustrated. A design revolution was under way.

But it was in Holland, not Germany, that the first major Modern design movement sprang up. Here in 1917 the group De Stijl, with its own magazine of the same name, was founded by Theo van Doesburg, architect and painter. The group included the famous non-representational painter Piet Mondrian and many architects, including J. J. P. Oud, Wilmos Huszar, Jan Wils, Robert van t'Hoff and Gerrit Rietveld. Van Doesburg had tremendous influence in Germany and Paris, but, apart from the paintings of Mondrian, it is the architecture and furniture of Rietveld which is best known today. Rietveld had been a cabinet-maker in Utrecht since 1911; in 1918 he produced his famous 'Red-Blue' chair of elementary form, painted, like Mondrian's canvases, in primary colours. In 1920 he evolved a hanging lamp of a revolutionary cubic shape, made of simple cubes of wood and lighting tubes, and in 1924 he designed his most famous building, a Modern house in Utrecht for the Schröder family.

Dutch design was one of the most important influences on the German Bauhaus, formed in 1919 when Walter Gropius was appointed to succeed Van de Velde as director of the Weimar School of Arts and Crafts. Renamed Das Staatliche Bauhaus Weimar, the school became an art college with distinctive Modern leanings. At first the old Muthesius-Van de Velde debate was re-enacted, with Gropius

64 Gerrit Rietveld: 'Red-Blue' chair in painted wood, designed and made in his own studios in Utrecht, 1918. One of the great classics of the De Stijl movement, based on the primary colours used by Piet Mondrian in his paintings.

playing the role of Muthesius and the painter Johannes Itten, who taught the basic course, that of the individualist Van de Velde. Then in 1921 and 1922 respectively, Paul Klee and Wassily Kandinsky were appointed by Gropius to teaching posts, and the Modern putsch was completed with the introduction of the Hungarian Constructivist Laszlo Moholy-Nagy in 1923. Itten left in the same year. The work of De Stijl had already had a marked effect: Gropius 'borrowed' the design of Rietveld's light fitting to use as his own, and Marcel Breuer, who taught woodwork, imitated Rietveld's geometric wooden furniture. The links were consolidated when, in 1921–2, Van Doesburg first lectured at the Bauhaus on De Stijl ideas. Five years later, Mart Stam, an independent Dutch architect who had 'invented' the first Modern tubular and metal cantilivered chair, was invited by the future Bauhaus director, Ludwig Mies van der Rohe, to contribute work to the 1927 Werkbund exhibition in Stuttgart. At about the same time Mies van der Rohe and Breuer both designed tubular steel chairs using industrial manufacturing processes.

Ideas of 'craft' at the Bauhaus were finally abandoned when Moholy-Nagy took over the metalwork studios and directed the

65 Walter Gropius: The Bauhaus building, Dessau, 1925. The flat roof, clean lines and white walls are all typical of the International Modern style.

66 Ludwig Mies van der Rohe: Tubular steel 'Weissenhof' chair, 1927.

students, particularly Marianne Brandt and Wilhelm Wagenfeld, towards a form of Modern industrial design. This transition can best be illustrated by comparing Brandt's teapot of 1924, which is geometric and Modern in form but made of silver and hand-hammered in a way that suggests a very late adherence to Arts and Crafts techniques, with her product-design light fittings of 1926 and 1927, industrially manufactured by Körting & Mathiesen of Leipzig.

These industrial gestures represented a final nail in the coffin for ornament and complemented the architectural requirements of the International Modern movement, which owed much to De Stijl and the Bauhaus but perhaps even more to the ideas of the Swiss-French architect Le Corbusier, who had worked alongside Gropius and Mies van der Rohe in Peter Behrens's office in 1910. Le Corbusier had begun as a painter working in a 'mechanical' style called Purism, which was derived from Cubism. In 1923 he wrote *Vers une architecture*, which urged everyone to live in a smaller flat than that of their

67 Ludwig Mies van der Rohe: Steel and leather 'Barcelona' chair and stool, 1929.

69 *(right)* Marianne Brandt: 'Kandem' table lamp, made by Körting & Mathiesen, Leipzig, 1928.

parents, and extolled the virtues of aeroplane and steamship design as well as the beauty of Greek architecture. Le Corbusier was really a modern classicist, though his *L'esprit nouveau* pavilion at the 1925 Paris Exhibition was a no-holds-barred version of Modernism, and he, too, designed tubular steel furniture, which was made by Thonet, a firm which had been famous for its bent-wood products in the nine-

70 *(right)* Marcel Breuer: Tubular steel chair designed at the Bauhaus, 1925.

68 *(below)* Marianne Brandt: Silver teapot designed and made at the Bauhaus metalwork studios under the direction of Laszlo Moholy-Nagy, 1924. An Arts and Crafts object which has a formalism inspired by Constructivism.

teenth century. The Stuttgart 1927 Exhibition provided a showcase for International Modern architecture: J. J. P. Oud, Mart Stam, Peter Behrens, Walter Gropius and Le Corbusier all contributed, showing their metal furniture and Marianne Brandt's light fittings. The very next year saw the first Congrès International d'Architecture Moderne (CIAM), organised by the Swiss critic Sigfried Giedion, later author of *Mechanisation Takes Command* (1948). International Modern architecture was born. It was to dominate building for the next decade.

It is perhaps significant that Le Corbusier's contribution to the 1925 Paris Exhibition was the most Modern work there. Indeed, the exhibition (Exposition Internationale des Arts Décoratifs et Industriels Modernes) gave its name to the alternative style known as Art Deco. France had been the leading centre of Art Nouveau, and Art Deco, which supplanted it, may be seen as an evolution from it as well as a reaction against it. Fauvism, Cubism and the presence of

Diaghilev's Ballets Russes all made their artistic contribution, as did the penchant for exotic tribalism already present in Picasso's early Cubist paintings. Art Deco continued the use of exotic materials such as lacquer, ivory and amboyna wood, but used Cubist forms to great effect. Leading furniture designers such as Jacques Emile Ruhlmann used tubular steel and yet adhered to a simplified form of classical design. France never forgot its sculptural tradition, and figure-drawing remained important in Art Deco. Jean Puiforçat, for example, was a sculptor before he became a silversmith, working in a style that owed much to classical geometry and a knowledge of the then fashionable Mexican ziggurat form. Art Deco still relied on superlative French standards of craftsmanship; unlike the Modern style it did not attempt to oust hand crafting in favour of the machine.

In England, both styles existed side by side, while Arts and Crafts furniture was still being produced. One has only to compare the bizarre, jazzy designs of Clarice Cliff with the simple engine-turned ceramics designed by Keith Murray for Wedgwood to grasp the extent of the gulf between Art Deco and Modern.

America's contribution during this period was to foster Inter-

71 *(above left)* Le Corbusier: 'Grand confort' armchair, designed with Pierre Jeanneret and Charlotte Perriand in 1925–8 for the Salon d'Automne, Paris.

72 *(above)* Pierre Turin: Bronze medal designed for the Exposition Internationale des Arts Décoratifs, Paris, 1925.

73 *(right)* Jacques Ruhlmann: Bureau, about 1925. An example of luxurious French Art Deco furniture.

74 *(below)* Jean Puiforçat: Silver tea-set, 1925.

75 *(left)* Frank Lloyd Wright:
Fallingwater, Bear Run,
Pennsylvania, 1936. Wright was
asked by Edgar Kaufmann Jr to
build this house for his father.

76 William van Alen: Chrysler
Building, New York, 1929, from
a painting by Chesley Bonestell,
about 1930. One of the greatest
New York 'Art Deco'
skyscrapers.

national Modern design and Art Deco simultaneously. While Frank Lloyd Wright's house Fallingwater, Bear Run, Pennsylvania (1936) is a tribute to International Modern architecture, William van Alen's Chrysler building (1929) is a New York version of Art Deco.

But it was in the realm of industrial and corporate design that America made its greatest impact. In the nineteenth century the United States had been responsible for inventions such as the telephone and the typewriter. The development and improvement of such innovations was as much an American achievement as good product design was a German one. The careers of Walter Teague, Norman Bel Geddes, Raymond Loewy, Henry Dreyfuss and Richard Buck-

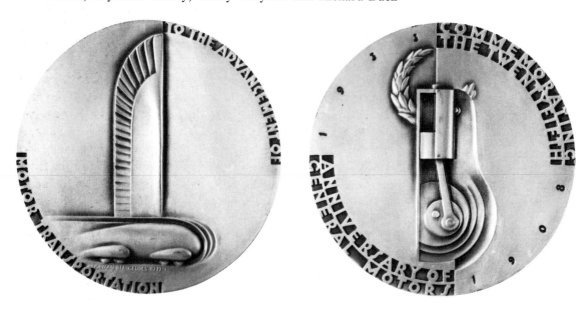

minster Fuller all took off in America in the late 1920s, at the same time as the Bauhaus was beginning to tackle mechanisation effectively.

Teague set up his design studio in 1926, and received his first important commission from Kodak in 1927; Bel Geddes took up industrial design in 1927, but his ideas for car bodies were not produced until the 1930s. Loewy redesigned the Gestetner duplicating machine in 1929; in the same year, Dreyfuss opened his design office and Buckminster Fuller conceived his Dymaxion car and Dymaxion house. In this technological, scientific modern approach, Fuller was less concerned with 'style' than the others and more interested in architecture. Between the wars, these men improved and generally 'streamlined' the design of aeroplanes, cars, cameras, telephones, refrigerators, stoves and railroad engines.

The strength of American interest in Modern design is shown by two events which took place in New York in 1934. In that year

77 Norman Bel Geddes: Medal commemorating the 25th anniversary of General Motors, 1933. An example of Bel Geddes' 'streamlining'.

Loewy's machine-style office was exhibited at the Metropolitan Museum, and the famous 'Machine Art' exhibition was held at the Museum of Modern Art. MOMA had been founded in 1929 and was from the beginning in favour only of uncompromisingly Modern design. It was the first museum to collect only Modern work as a matter of policy, swiftly overtaking all other institutions in that respect. The 'Machine Art' exhibition revealed, in Platonic terms, the 'ideal' beauty of the ball bearing, propeller blade and coil spring. This reductionist approach was not unique to America or to design: in Britain in the same year Raymond McGrath published his book *Twentieth-Century Houses*, which was written in 'basic English' with a severely restricted vocabulary, and one might argue that George Orwell's writing reflects the same trend. But in design, at least, the idea can be traced back to the 1924 Werkbund 'Form without Ornament' exhibition.

Both England and, later, America benefited from the presence of some Bauhaus 'stars' in their midst, refugees from Nazi Germany. The school had been persecuted by the Nazis and was finally dissolved in 1933. Some English design writers and practitioners were already very sensitive to Modernity; they included Herbert Read, J. M. Richards and Jack 'Plywood' Pritchard, as well as a band of International Modern architects, most of whom were of British colonial origin: Wells Coates, the aforementioned Raymond McGrath, Amyas Connell, Basil Ward and Colin Lucas. The presence of the refugees from the Bauhaus – Moholy-Nagy, Breuer and the great Gropius – as well as that of other International Modern architects such as Berthold Lubetkin and Erich Mendelsohn, strengthened the cause. Britain formed its own Modern Architectural Research Group (MARS) in 1934 and there was even talk of starting a New Bauhaus in England. In the event, this was destined to happen in America, which was more surely the land of the Modern. Gropius and Breuer left England for Harvard in 1937, and Moholy-Nagy became director of the New Bauhaus in Chicago in the same year. Mies van der Rohe went to Illinois in 1938, without the intermediate stage of a limited sojourn in England.

Industrial design had improved greatly in Britain between the wars, but for the most part this was in the wake of the lead established by Germany and the USA. Exceptions, such as R. J. Mitchell's brilliant design for an aircraft which eventually became the Spitfire, are few and far between, and it may be argued that the Arts and Crafts tradition survived in Britain for a very long time. For instance, as late as 1942, when during the war a design for mass furniture became necessary, Gordon Russell was dragged away from stone-carving in the Cotswolds to supervise the production of Utility furniture in

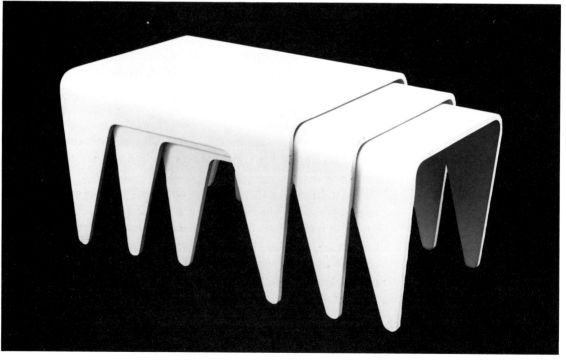

80 *(above)* Marcel Breuer: Plywood 'long chair' for the Isokon group, 1936.

78 *(above left)* Alvar Aalto: Plywood table and stools, made by Finmar, about 1938. A gentle interpretation of Modern design.

79 *(left)* Marcel Breuer: Plywood stacking tables designed for Jack Pritchard's Isokon group, 1936. During his brief stay in England, Breuer experimented with plywood furniture.

London. The result was still Arts and Crafts in spirit and was considered 'retrograde' by the International Modern *Architectural Review*.

If it was difficult to thrust Britain into the Modern world, gargantuan problems faced the Soviet Union after the 1917 Revolution. Suddenly, this industrially backward country with its excellent craft tradition found itself hurled headlong into the twentieth century. Artists took the lead in this, among them El Lissitzky. Lissitzky had studied engineering and architecture at Darmstadt, where one of his teachers was Olbrich. The Revolution, in which Lissitzky took an active part, made artists think about the challenge of the new age and new economic requirements. In 1919 Lissitzky became involved with Suprematism, a form of abstract art invented by Kasimir Malevich,

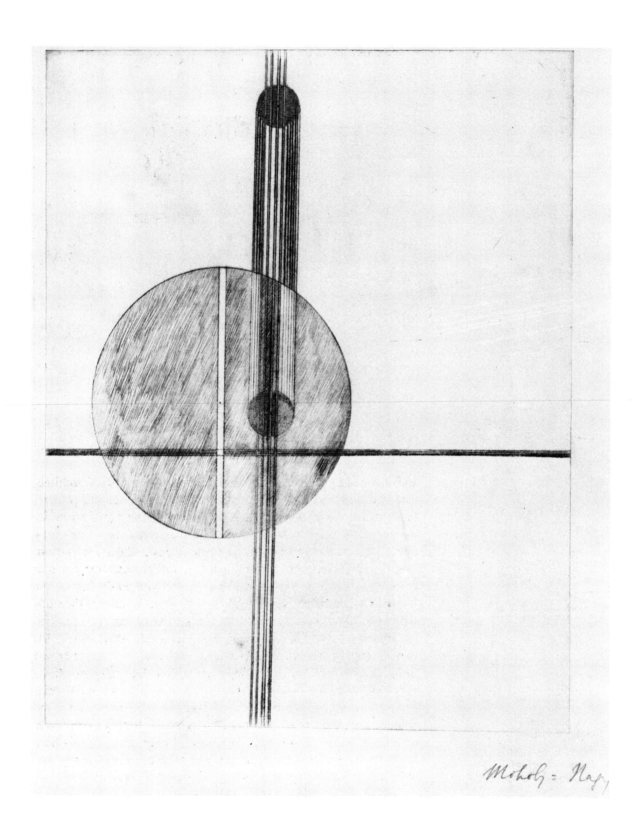

Moholy-Nagy

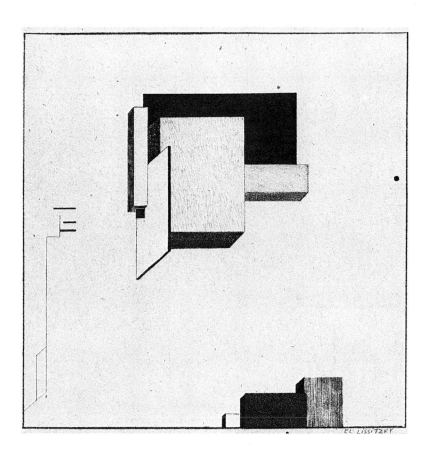

82 *(right)* El Lissitzky: *Proun
IC*. Lithograph, 1919–21.
Russian Constructivist art of the
Revolutionary period.

81 Laszlo Moholy-Nagy:
Suprematisch. Drypoint, 1924.
An interpretation of
Constructivism, made at the
Bauhaus.

and obtained a post at Vitebsk, where he taught graphics and architecture and designed pro-Revolutionary children's books and posters. He also became involved in the PROUN movement (a 'Project for the Affirmation of the New') and from 1920 worked on his visionary design for the Lenin Platform, a massive crane-like aerial podium from which he imagined Lenin might speak. The next year saw him teaching at the Vhkutemas in Moscow, a Soviet equivalent of the Bauhaus, where he worked with Vladimir Tatlin, founder of the Constructivist movement. Lissitzky returned to Germany in 1921, and in Düsseldorf met Moholy-Nagy, who was much influenced by his ideas. Lissitzky had many international contacts; in 1922 he edited the *Object/Veshch/Gegenstand/Objet* periodical in Berlin, inviting contributions from Van Doesburg and Le Corbusier. In 1924 he met Mart Stam in Zurich, and designed Bauhaus-style graphics for the German firm Pelikan Ink. He returned to Moscow in 1925 as Professor of Design at the Vhkutemas, only to travel again in 1926, this time to study new Dutch architecture. Although he designed a few pieces of furniture, Lissitzky was primarily a designer of graphics.

His colleague at the Vhkutemas, Tatlin, is best known for his vast

83 Vladimir Tatlin: Monument
to the Third International, 1920
(reconstruction made in 1971).

maquette for a monument to the Third International in 1920 and
his designs for easy-to-wear workers' clothing in 1923. Similar projects for 'revolutionary' clothes were produced by the artists Liobov
Popova and Alexander Rodtchenko. The latter also designed Modern
furniture. Apart from theatre and graphic design, few Soviet projects
reached the level of achievement or output of the German Bauhaus,
and yet, as 'work in progress', Soviet art was extremely fertile. The
most important work was produced at the Vhutein, successor to the
Vhkutemas, for example Modern folding chairs, using wood and
metal, by B. P. Zemlianitsyn and a Modern bent-wood chair by
N. N. Rogozhin (1928).

However, it was in ceramics that the Soviet Union made its greatest
contribution to Modern design. After the Revolution, porcelain from
the Lomonossov factory under Sergei Chekhonin was at first painted
with 'agitprop', new Soviet slogans on old forms. But soon entirely
Modern forms were produced – 'mechanical' in feeling and abstract
in decoration – by the two Suprematist artists Kasimir Malevich and
Nikolai Suetin. Their designs are amongst the few totally successful
integrations of ceramics and Modern art, the best being a porcelain
inkstand by Suetin, dating from 1923.

84 Alexander Rodtchenko:
Chess table, 1925. A Soviet
experiment which parallels the
work of the Bauhaus.

85 Sergei Chekhonin: Porcelain plate painted with a Russian Revolutionary slogan, made at the Lomonossov porcelain factory, Petrograd, about 1921. The plate commemorates October 1917, and the slogan can be translated 'Victory of working people'. See also Plate VI.

In the 1920s these Constructivist, Suprematist and abstract experiments flourished in the Soviet Union alongside revolutionary Modern architecture. But much work, like that of Iakov Chernikhov, remained only on paper, and in any case the death of Lenin and the replacement under Stalin of abstraction by an easily understood folk realism followed rapidly. Modernism was destroyed more completely by Stalin than it was by Hitler in Germany, although under these dictators in the 1930s both countries turned to an inflated neo-classicism in their architecture. We have seen that neo-classicism had in any case remained an important source of inspiration for Modern architects such as Behrens and Mies van der Rohe, both of whom were influenced by Schinkel, but they took it less literally than, for example, the Austrian architect Adolf Loos. In Nazi Germany architects like Albert Speer worked extensively in this style, which can also be seen, with even grander pomp, in the Moscow Metro of Stalin's period.

It is incorrect, however, to assume that Modern design was obliterated in Germany after the closure of the Bauhaus by the Nazis. Mies van der Rohe, and even Gropius to some extent, had at first attempted a compromise with the new regime, and the designers Wilhelm Wagenfeld and Hermann Gretsch did some of their best

86 Wilhelm Wagenfeld: Set of
glass stacking jars and dishes, for
the Vereinigte Lausitzer
Glaswerke, Weisswasser, 1938.

87 Wilhelm Wagenfeld: Glass
teapot made by Schott und Gen.
Jena Glaswerke, 1934. The
Bauhaus attempted to lighten
design, and Wagenfeld took this
aim literally.

work during the Nazi period. Ferdinand Porsche's Volkswagen design was actually approved by Hitler in 1936. Yet in the same year, when Moholy-Nagy returned to Berlin to retrieve some of his 'abstract' works which had been left with his housekeeper, the latter told him that he had destroyed them and threatened to denounce him as a cultural bolshevik. Attitudes to art and design are often paradoxical, but never more so than during this turbulent period.

During the 1930s, therefore, neo-classicism was associated with Stalin and Hitler and the reputation of a-political architects who practised the style suffered as a result. One such was the great British architect Sir Edwin Lutyens, whose name hardly appeared in any assessment of design until recently. Lutyens was in his own way something of a rebel, having been attracted from as early as 1894 to the William and Mary style and to neo-classicism, although, like almost everyone else, he also continued to work in the prevailing Arts and Crafts idiom. He offended Dame Henrietta Barnett by producing neo-Georgian and neo-William and Mary houses for Hampstead Garden Suburb from 1908, going against the preference she had expressed for Arts and Crafts architecture. In the same year he submitted a design for the London County Hall. The competition was in the event won by Ralph Knott, and the building was completed in 1922 in a neo-classical style that continued to be seen as appropriate for civic architecture, a 'polite' style largely untouched by the real Modern movement.

As a designer, Lutyens is extraordinarily prophetic of Post-Modernism, although his materials of course remain those of his own day. His ability to use wit, symbol, metaphor and even 'anti-design' anticipates Post-Modernism by half a century. For example, he designed a movable garden seat for Ednaston Manor (built in 1912) which has a wheel and handles that make it look like a wheelbarrow. This foreshadows Bruno Minardi's whimsical designs for garden furniture in painted iron, designed in 1985 and made in Italy, which could be labelled 'Post-Modern Classical'. Lutyens's garden seat is, however, made of wood, and he himself would not have welcomed the comparison. His nursery light fittings for the Viceroy's House, New Delhi, designed between 1927 and 1930, are playful jokes: as his daughter Mary recalls in her book, *Edwin Lutyens* (1980), 'he had particular fun with his designs for the nursery chandeliers, all of brightly painted wood, one showing four angels praying to a starlit globe, another four prancing horses, and a third four hens, with their chicks, who had just laid eggs: hanging from the four arms of this wooden structure broken egg-shells split their joke (their yoke) in the form of light bulbs. All his gaiety, inventiveness, ingenuity and lightness of touch are revealed in these chandeliers.' Lutyens's clock for

88 Hermann Gretsch: Porcelain coffee pot made by Porzellanfabrik Arzberg, Bavaria, 1931. A classic of Modern design, which is still in production.

the same house is urn-shaped, with two brass handles. It stands on four bun feet and has expanding lazy tongs for 'hands'. The top itself has a brass winding key in the form of a shamrock inside a miniature urn; and the whole clock is painted pale marbled blue. If produced today it might be labelled Post-Modern, but it is of course anti-Modern. Nothing would have offended the contemporary 1930s rationalists more than this whimsical and humorous clock.

A popular target for the cartoonists of his day, Lutyens even went so far as to caricature himself in a light fitting. His famous owl glasses, pith helmet and pipe are all referred to in his saucer-shaped light fittings for New Delhi; the saucer combines the brim of his pith hat with the shape of the base of a type of dome much used by him in India; the cage echoes Lutyens's glasses, and the tassel his pipe. The same fitting was used in the chapel of Campion Hall, built for the Jesuits in Oxford between 1935 and 1942, and has been likened to a cardinal's hat with tassels. Nikolaus Pevsner wrote of Lutyens's 'retrograde style' and it is significant that his work appeals to conservative critics and conservationists.

Lutyens gave much encouragement to other designers and architects, among them Oliver Hill, noteworthy for his conversion from a Lutyens-based classicism and 'vogue Regency' style to a form of Modernism. Lutyens himself had designed 'Queen Anne' and 'Regency' revival chairs for the Viceroy's House in India, while Hill was capable of producing a design for a wheel-backed eighteenth-century revival chair in 1929, as well as furniture for Heal and Son that looks like a British version of Art Deco 'Moderne'. As we shall see when we come to look at Post-Modernism, this revivalism that sprang up between the wars is now being taken seriously again, after a long period of neglect as a result of the dominance of its bitter enemy, the International Modern style. After the high Germanic seriousness of much Bauhaus work, it is a welcome change to find humour in the work of men who did not think of themselves as prophets.

89 Edwin Lutyens: Metal light fitting with tassels, designed for the Viceroy's House, New Delhi, about 1930. An example of Lutyens's humour in design, with an element of self-caricature.

COLLEGE LIBRARY
COLLEGE OF TECHNOLOGY
CARNARVON ROAD
SOUTHEND-ON-SEA. ESSEX

4 FREE FLOW
THE 1950s

The Second World War interrupted design developments in Europe, but America, which entered the war only in 1941, produced some of its most exciting work between 1940 and 1945. In 1940 Eliot Noyes was appointed first director of the Museum of Modern Art's department of industrial design, and he was succeeded after the war by Edgar Kaufmann Jr. Kaufmann had already been responsible for persuading his father to commission Frank Lloyd Wright to design his house Fallingwater in 1936. He also did much to promote purist design. For example, he attacked Thirties-style streamlining in an article entitled 'Borax, or the Chromium-Plated Calf', which appeared in the *Architectural Review* in 1948.

Both Noyes and Kaufmann continued MOMA's 1930s tradition of sponsoring good design. We saw in Chapter 3 that a New Bauhaus, under Moholy-Nagy, was started in Chicago. It failed, but in 1939 Moholy-Nagy opened his own school, which in 1944 became known as the Chicago Institute of Design. There he continued to use Bauhaus teaching methods, but with a stronger interest in 'organic' forms, especially 'hand-sculpture' (he had done some sculpture himself in the 1930s). The importance of sculpture in the development of the Fifties style will be noted often in this chapter.

An earlier precedent for a European-style design college in the United States had been set by another European, Eliel Saarinen, who arrived in America from Finland in 1923, not as a refugee but in the wake of much praise for his architectural entry for the 1922 Chicago Tribune Tower competition. He had been commissioned to build the Cranbrook school for boys near Detroit, and in 1929 he also designed the Cranbrook school for girls at nearby Kingswood. In 1932 he was appointed President of the Cranbrook Academy of Art. Saarinen and his wife Loja also designed furnishings, and in this they were followed by their son, Eero. Eero Saarinen's career is particularly interesting in the light of 1950s design developments; he trained to be a sculptor in Paris in 1930–31 before becoming an architect and working on furniture design with Norman Bel Geddes.

The younger Saarinen returned to Cranbrook in 1936, where he taught with Charles Eames, Harry Bertoia and Florence Schust. Eames had also joined Cranbrook in 1936; Bertoia arrived in 1937 and taught metalwork and jewellery there from 1939. All were influential in shaping the development of furniture design in the 1950s. Florence Schust married Hans Knoll, of the well-known German furniture firm, in 1946. The firm had produced good furniture since the First World War, and Hans Knoll had emigrated to America in 1935 and established a successful branch there. He employed Saarinen, Eames and Bertoia to design for him, and the combination of the 'Cranbrook three' and an enlightened manufacturer proved a fruitful one.

In 1940 Eames and Saarinen won prizes for their plywood chair designs in the Museum of Modern Art's 'Organic Design in Home Furnishings' competition. The selection committee included Edgar Kaufmann Jr and Eliot Noyes as well as the Bauhaus designer Marcel Breuer, who had himself designed some 'organic' furniture during his short period in England, for Jack 'Plywood' Pritchard's Isokon group. Noyes defined 'organic' as the 'harmonious organisation of the parts within the whole, according to structure, material and purpose. Within this definition there can be no vain ornamentation or superfluity, but the part of beauty is none the less great – in ideal choice of material, in visual refinement and in the rational elegance of things intended for use.' MOMA continued to sponsor 'good design' throughout the decade, and in 1948 organised an 'International Competition for Low-Cost Furniture', in which Eames was awarded second prize for his fibreglass chair by a jury consisting of Kaufmann, Mies van der Rohe and the Briton Gordon Russell. Many of the names which were to be famous in the 1950s entered for this competition, including Ernest Race and Robin Day from England, the Scandinavian Jørn Utzon and the Italians Gino Columbini, Marco Zanuso and Franco Albini. The Fifties style was beginning to take shape.

However, in the 1940s Eames, Bertoia and Saarinen remained the most important innovators. Eames moved to California in 1941 and worked with moulded plywood, producing leg splints for the US Navy and – from 1943, when Bertoia joined him – aircraft sections, adapting a technology wrought from British experiments with the light but strong plywood warplane, the Mosquito. Out of this came Eames's brilliant plywood-backed chair, with splayed legs of chromed steel, of 1945, and a curvy plywood screen of 1946, followed by his fibreglass and steel chair of 1948. It was mainly from these forms that the organic, spindly style of the 1950s developed, though it also had precedents in the late 1930s. In 1937 the Italian Gio Ponti had designed a chair on spindly legs, and in the same year Alvar Aalto had produced

90 Alvar Aalto: Glass vase for Iittala, 1937. The organic quality of this glass heralded the style of the 1950s.

91 Alvar Aalto: Entrance of the
Paimio Sanatorium, Finland,
1929–33.

92 Eero Saarinen: Fibreglass-
reinforced plastic 'Womb' chair
and stool for Knoll Associates,
1946. An 'organic' design typical
of the immediate post-war
period.

93 Harry Bertoia: 'Diamond' wing chair in steel wire, 1951–2.

94 Eero Saarinen: Plastic and aluminium 'Tulip' table and chairs for Knoll Associates, 1957.

95 Hans Arp, *Mask*. Wood engraving, 1948. An organic palette shape which anticipates 1950s free-form design.

a wavy 'free-form' glass for Iittala in Finland, its shape inspired by the indentations of a fjord.

Eames's work was followed by Saarinen's highly sculptural 'Womb' chair of 1946 and Bertoia's 'Diamond' chair of 1952. Plywood, fibreglass and steel lent themseves to organic, free-form treatment, and these chairs set a standard in the use of these newer materials for other designers and craftsmen to emulate. In 1946, for example, Eva Zeisel produced, through MOMA's patronage, her 'Museum' ceramic set, which is as much an example of early Fifties design as it is an extension of Thirties Modern movement 'good form'. In the late 1920s and 1930s, before going to America, Zeisel, who trained in her native Hungary, worked in German ceramic companies and at Lomonossov in the Soviet Union.

One of Eames's chairs, designed in 1948, was asymmetrical in form

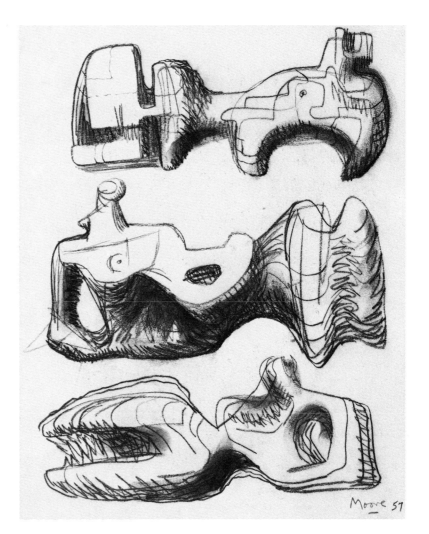

96 Henry Moore: *Three drawings of sculpture*, 1957. Moore's sculpture of the 1930s foreshadowed free-form design, and his work of the 1950s retains a strongly organic quality.

and contained a hole, like contemporary sculpture by Hans Arp, Henry Moore and Barbara Hepworth. The free-form shapes created by these sculptors, and also the use of string and nylon in the work of another, Naum Gabo, were well known and evidently admired by aspiring designers after the Second World War. Sculpture was indeed to have a profound effect on ceramics, glass and metalwork as well as furniture during the 1950s. The German designer Beate Kuhn, for example, produced Hepworth-like free-form ceramics, with white interiors, dark exteriors and holes in them, for the innovative German firm Rosenthal, which after the war pursued an intelligent, entrepreneurial policy towards international design. Rosenthal commissioned the American 'streamline' designer Raymond Loewy to design a coffee service with Richard Latham in 1954. Even Walter Gropius was asked to design a tea service: the result was bulging in

97 *(left)* Arne Jacobsen: 'Egg' chair and stool, made by Fritz Hansens, 1958.

98 *(right)* Beate Kuhn: Porcelain vases designed for Rosenthal, about 1953.

99 *(below)* Raymond Loewy and Richard Latham: Porcelain coffee set '2000' for Rosenthal, 1954.

form, but sculptural and streamlined, thus marrying two Fifties tendencies. It was called 'TACI' and produced in 1959. These Rosenthal sets are characteristic of the 1950s in their emphasis on the curve. However, the style was not universally admired. The more purist, Bauhaus-trained designer Wilhelm Wagenfeld, himself once admonished by his teacher Moholy-Nagy for not being pure enough, wrote in 1954, 'The kidney table (i.e. free-form design) is certainly no more attractive than Chippendale reproductions so much favoured by our Philistines, and the Rococo vases adorned with brightly-coloured transfer pictures no more absurd than the asymmetrical knick-knacks of today.'

It is clear, then, that by 1954 Wagenfeld, at least, perceived that the essence of this new style was 'free-form'. As we shall see, all over the design world this style emerged from the more functionalist tradition of the 1930s to which Wagenfeld belonged. Its exponents included Gio Ponti, Lino Sabattini and Paolo Venini in Italy, and Søren Georg Jensen, Henning Koppel, Timo Sarpaneva and Tapio Wirkkala in Scandinavia.

Work in Italy and Scandinavia is indeed often thought to be of primary importance in the development of European design after the war, while American work is unjustly overlooked. Italy, the country

100 Walter Gropius: 'TACI' porcelain teapot, cup and saucer for Rosenthal, 1959. The surface decoration was designed later by Gropius's former Bauhaus colleague Herbert Bayer.

of the Renaissance, made surprisingly little contribution to nineteenth-century design; it even called its Art Nouveau style *stile Liberty* for want of a better, indigenous title. In 1928, however, the architect Gio Ponti founded *Domus*, one of the first Modern design magazines. He also lent his weight to the design Biennales (later Triennales), first at Monza (1923–30) and then in Milan, which was destined to become the foremost design city of Italy. Among Ponti's most famous products are the 'bulging' La Pavone coffee machine of 1949 and a washbasin and lavatory of 1953 and 1954 which wed classical purity with a slight Fifties curve.

One of Ponti's admirers was the silversmith Lino Sabattini, who had educated himself in Como by reading *Domus*, and who produced

101 Gio Ponti: Metal and glass table made by Fontana, Italy, about 1950.

work with characteristic Fifties bulge forms, for example his aptly named 'Boule' teapot of 1950. Sabattini moved to Milan in 1955 and established contact with Ponti and his circle. Ponti encouraged Sabattini, who continued to produce free-form designs, such as his 'Como' service of 1957, made by Christofle in France.

Paolo Venini, the famous Italian glass designer, worked with Ponti from as early as 1927. Venini's most celebrated contribution to the Fifties style was his much-imitated 'Handkerchief' glass of 1949, a hand-blown glass of spiky, asymmetrical free form, made at his works in Murano. This set a new standard for the prolific Scandinavian designers, already inspired by Alvar Aalto's glass of 1937. The Finnish designer Tapio Wirkkala was from 1947 chief designer for Iittala. His free-form 'Kanttarelli' glass of 1947 and sea-anemone-like glass bowl of 1953 are both organic in design and shape. Wirkkala also made plywood bowls in the early 1950s, and his metalwork, often using leaf forms, is usually gently asymmetrical. Leaf forms were a *leitmotif* of 1950s textile design and furniture decoration. In the mid-1950s

102 Lino Sabattini: Electroplate 'Como' tea and coffee service for Christofle, Paris, 1957.

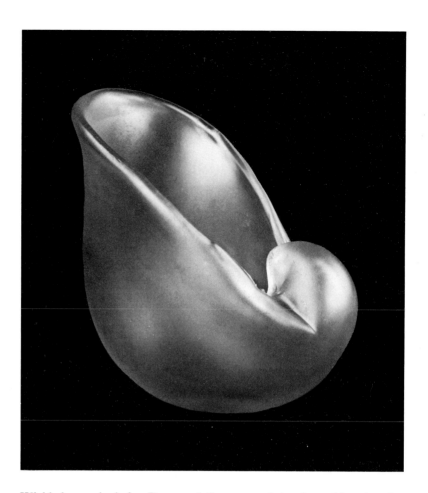

103 Paolo Venini: Glass vase, made by his own firm about 1950.

Wirkkala worked for Raymond Loewy and in the mid-1960s for Venini. Another Finn, Timo Sarpaneva, who trained in Helsinki, also worked for Iittala from 1950. He, too, worked in glass, and in 1954 designed what might be called a free-form glass sculpture, with a hole in it. This form was named 'the most beautiful object of the year' by *House Beautiful*. In that same year he won a prize at the influential Milan Triennale. A third important Scandinavian glass designer was the Swede Vicke Lindstrand, who had worked at Orrefors in the 1930s and became design director at Kosta in 1950. Like Sarpaneva, his work included pierced and sculpted glass.

No account of Scandinavian design would be complete without reference to Georg Jensen, a firm of Copenhagen silversmiths who were extremely influential in establishing a 'house-style' of 'good form'. The founder, Georg Arthur Jensen, had worked in a style which blended the traditions of Arts and Crafts and Art Nouveau; in the 1930s Johan Rohde had reflected the functionalist aesthetic of the decade in his simple metalwork. In the late 1940s the style changed

104 *(left)* Tapio Wirkkala:
'Tapio' glasses for Iittala, 1954.

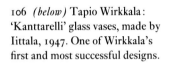

105 *(right)* Tapio Wirkkala:
Porcelaine noire teapot for
Rosenthal, about 1960.

106 *(below)* Tapio Wirkkala:
'Kanttarelli' glass vases, made by
Iittala, 1947. One of Wirkkala's
first and most successful designs.

again with work by Henning Koppel, who, like so many other designers of this period, had been trained as a sculptor. The amoeba-like forms of his jewellery were characteristic of the age, and represented a new departure for the Jensen firm. They are reminiscent of flattened versions of Hans Arp's sculpture and their jigsaw-like shapes, sometimes enamelled, give easy pleasure to the eye. Koppel began to design hollow- and flatware in the 1950s, winning gold medals at the Milan Triennales of 1951 and 1957, and he fulfilled his ambition of producing silver which was 'useful, and a joy to behold'. His swollen silver teapot with ivory handle of 1954 and his fish-shaped dish of the same year are perhaps the two most famous pieces of metalwork to emerge during the decade.

Koppel was followed in this style by Søren Georg Jensen, son of the founder of the firm. Like Koppel some ten years before him, Jensen had studied sculpture at the Royal Danish Academy of Fine Arts, and in 1951 he produced an exciting gourd-shaped condiment set for the family enterprise. Its sweeping curve was very much in keeping with the new Fifties style.

The internationalism of the Fifties style was as far-reaching as that of the Modernism from which it had evolved. The work of the American-Japanese designer Isamu Noguchi is a good example: he trained for a while in Constantin Brancusi's Paris studio, and in the 1940s designed a highly sculptural plate-glass table on a walnut base, which is reminiscent of the work of Henry Moore, particularly his sculpture of 1939 *Three Points* (Tate Gallery, London). However, Noguchi adopted a more traditionally Japanese idiom for his later white paper lampshades.

Perhaps the most striking volte-face in the crafts can be seen in the work of the Dutch glass artist Andries Copier, whose severe work for the Leerdam factory in the 1930s had been almost entirely inspired by the Modern movement; by the 1950s he, too, was producing free-form work with flowing shapes.

The 'bulge' style of the 1950s also had an influence on the design of cars, which continued to be streamlined or to follow 'airflow' shapes. The 1950 Saab car, for example, combined the shape of an aircraft cockpit with the general impression of a large hand-sculpture on wheels. Much the same can be said for many cars of the mid-1950s, for example the Jaguar in England or the Citroën in France.

In architecture, too, there were dramatic changes in direction from some of the greatest 'functionalist' architects of the 1930s. Frank Lloyd Wright's abandonment of rigid geometric forms came quite early in his planning of the spiral concrete Guggenheim Museum in New York, begun in 1943 but only completed in 1959. Equally significant was Le Corbusier's failing interest in his own functionalist ideas

107 Eero Saarinen: TWA
building, New York, 1961,
showing Saarinen's expressive
use of architectural form.

107 Eero Saarinen: TWA
building, New York, 1961,
showing Saarinen's expressive
use of architectural form.

of the preceding decades. His famous church of Notre-Dame-du-Haut at Ronchamp, begun in 1950 and completed in 1955, still used concrete, but its upswept curves and plasticity were entirely Fifties gestures.

Eero Saarinen, who has already been mentioned in connection with Cranbrook, also used curves in his architecture, for instance his shell-concrete roof for the Auditorium Building at Massachusetts Institute of Technology (1952). His TWA terminal at Kennedy Airport, New York, of 1961, with its use of concrete in organic, free-flowing shapes, is another monument to the rejection of the geometric Modernism of the Bauhaus era. Its upswept curves fittingly suggest flight and are perhaps the most extreme statement of the 'airborne' influence in Fifties architecture. Another is the much-discussed Sydney Opera

House by Jørn Utzon, with its expressionistic sail-like shell roofs, begun in 1957.

108 Jørn Utzon: Sydney Opera House, begun in 1957.

An assessment of Britain's contribution to the decade has been left until last. Shattered by the war, Britain made a desperate effort to assume the role of the phoenix. The 'Britain can make it' exhibition held at the Victoria & Albert Museum in 1946 was the first attempt at a show of strength, though there was something faintly embarrassing about the actual designs, which included a pneumatic chair developed from wartime 'inflatables'. The wartime mentality even hung over Ernest Race's excellent iron and plywood dining-room suite, which contained his 'BA' chair, designed in 1945 as a means of recycling scrap metal, particularly aluminium alloy. The chair later won

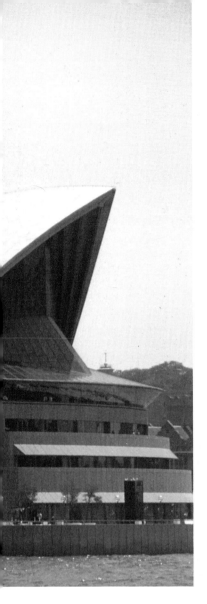

a gold medal at the 1951 Milan Triennale. The subject of design generated much discussion and many committees, but as so often seems to happen in England, little *élan* as a result. However, in 1948 Robin Darwin was appointed Principal of the Royal College of Art and serious design education was given full weight at this high level; by 1951 the college was awarding its Des. RCA qualification.

The Festival of Britain, held on the South Bank in 1951, was a perfect reflection of the mood of the period. The whole Festival site was laid out by 'Modern' architects: its more memorable structures, now gone, included the Dome of Discovery by Ralph Tubbs and the futuristic Skylon by Powell and Moya. Whimsy and serious design co-existed side by side: Ernest Race produced interesting and characteristically spindly chairs called 'Springbok' for the Festival site; they share some of the free-form thinness of his equally aptly named 'Antelope' chairs, also designed for the Festival, in 1950.

The best building on the site, the Festival Hall, still stands as witness to the event. Designed by Sir Robert Matthew and Sir Leslie Martin, it has many features typical of its time, including a free-flow interior, greater use of colour than would have been possible in the previous decade, and an upswept roof.

In terms of design, Britain produced little which will stand comparison with the work of the 'Cranbrook three' in America; indeed,

109 Ernest Race: Cabinet in iron, plywood and aluminium, 1945, designed en suite with his 'BA' chair as a means of recycling aluminium from wartime scrap.

111 Festival of
Britain Yachting
Regattas medal, 1951,
incorporating the
Festival logo.

110 *(left)* Festival of Britain
medal, 1951, showing the Festival
site. To the right are the Dome of
Discovery and the Skylon.

112 Ernest Race: 'Antelope'
chairs made by his own firm for
the Festival of Britain, 1951.

113 Robin Day: 'Hillestack' plywood stacking chair, 1950.

the talents of one of the best furniture designers of the decade, Robin Day, were only recognised in 1948 as a result of a visit by the directors of Hille, a traditional furniture firm, to America, where they saw Day's winning entry for MOMA's 'Low-Cost Furniture' competition. Day's career is typical of the period: he trained at the Royal College of Art from 1935 to 1939 and opened a freelance practice in London with his designer wife, Lucienne, in 1948. The discovery of his work in New York brought him commissions for Hille, which was anxious to develop its business towards 'new' furniture. In 1949 the company asked Day and his colleague Clive Latimer to design furniture for exhibition at the British Industry Fair, and in 1950 Day became Hille's 'house' designer. He designed their offices and produced a brilliant plywood stacking chair for them, the 'Hillestack'. Its use of plywood and inverted V-shaped splayed legs is characteristic of the period. In 1951 Day was commissioned to design seating for the Festival Hall, and in the same year he put together an individual 'selection' for the Milan Triennale. The room contained his own excellent furniture, modern ceramics, sculpture by Reg Butler and Henry Moore and a superb printed cotton fabric designed by his wife, Lucienne, and produced by Heal Fabrics. With its free-form abstract design, this fabric, called 'Calyx', was one of the best textiles of the time. Day's room won him the gold medal at the Triennale, and throughout the 1950s he continued to design excellent award-winning furniture, culminating in his famous polypropylene stacking chair for Hille in 1961.

Meanwhile, the efforts made in the late 1940s to revitalise the Royal College of Art were paying dividends. The 1950s generation of students included the silversmiths Eric Clements, Gerald Benney, Robert Welch and David Mellor. All paid homage to the Fifties 'bulge' style in their silversmithing, while also thinking about design for mass-production. This transition from craft to 'design' parallels that which took place in Scandinavia in the 1950s; and it may be argued that it was not until the 1960s that British craftsmen began to make contributions to product design at a major level. Eric Clements's free-flow silverware of the early 1950s is impressive in its rhythms, a particularly fine example being the tea-set commissioned by the Tea Centre to commemorate the Coronation in 1953. Gerald Benney's curvy tea-set of 1952, which sits on splayed legs rather like those of Day's chairs, is a splendid example of Fifties style; it is illustrated, together with its silver-lined walnut tray, alongside contemporary Scandinavian work in the influential *Studio Year Book of Decorative Art* for 1955. Benney's vessels of the late 1950s, which

114 Gerald Benney: Silver coffee pot, 1958. The curve of the lid is characteristic of the 1950s.

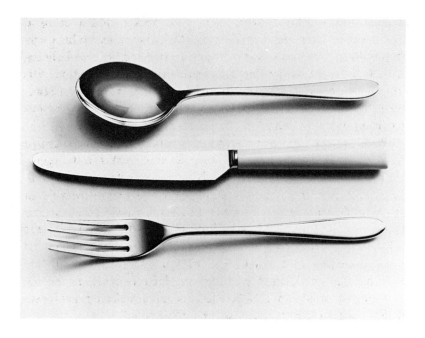

115 David Mellor: 'Pride' electroplate cutlery for Walker & Hall, 1954.

have upswept curved lids echoing the Festival Hall roof, adopted an idiom which was very much of the decade.

Robert Welch and David Mellor were more concerned with 'design', as opposed to the craft of silversmithing. Both continued to use silver, but increasingly looked towards other materials for mass-production. Welch had travelled in Scandinavia in 1953–4 and became very interested in stainless steel. In 1957 he collaborated with David Mellor to produce the 'Campden' range of flatware. Mellor's 'Pride'

116 David Mellor: 'Embassy' silver condiment set, designed for British embassies, 1963.

range of cutlery in silver-plate, designed for Walker and Hall in 1954, is an excellent example of good design. He chose to set up his work-shop in Sheffield, where he had begun his training, thus underlining the city's traditional associations with cutlery manufacture. His hollow-ware of the 1950s has much of the flow characteristic of Scan-dinavian work of the period, and this is retained in the hand-sculpture-like forms of his 'Embassy' condiment set of the mid-1960s.

The change of attitude in favour of product and industrial design was largely created in response to the widening market in the 1960s, as will be seen in the next chapter. Britain's contribution to style in the 1950s was relatively limited and came very much in the wake of American developments in furniture and Scandinavian developments in design. Peter Porter tellingly satirises the period in his poem 'Made in Heaven' (1961), which begins 'From Heals and Harrods come her lovely bridegrooms' and contains witty period references to 'the craftsman-felt wood, Swedish dressers, the labour-saving kitchen, the stereophonic radiogram'. As Harold Macmillan's election manifesto of 1957 suggested, Britain had 'never had it so good'.

5 POP AND LIQUORICE ALLSORTS
THE 1960s TO POST-MODERNISM

In the last chapter, we saw that 1950s design was in the main sculptural, free flowing and organic. In reaction to this, by the late 1950s, square forms began to oust rounded ones, much as they had after 1914 as a reaction against Art Nouveau. These changes are even reflected in the preferred shape of the female body. A Rubensian type was in vogue before 1914; the 1920s saw the advent of the boyish flapper by way of contrast. The universally admired image of the 1950s was the curvaceous Jayne Russell, while the 1960s were represented by the thin Jean Shrimpton and even thinner Twiggy. Such cyclical patterns also existed in the eighteenth century, with echoes in changes in design style.

Alec Issigonis's design for the 'jellymould' Morris Minor car of 1948 was suitably round; his famous Mini of 1959 was flatter and more angular. Also in 1959, the Italian Ettore Sottsass designed the Olivetti Tekne 3 typewriter, which was rectilinear in contrast to the still rounded IBM Executive by Eliot Noyes of the same date. The absolute rectilinearity of Hans Gugelot and Dieter Rams's famous Braun record-player of 1962, the Phonosuper SK4, nicknamed 'Snow White's Coffin', underlined this change. We shall see that two of the dominant art movements of the 1960s, Op Art and Minimalism, used strong geometric elements, while a third, Pop Art, remained a force running counter to the concept of 'good' design.

Op (optical) Art took its inspiration from earlier experiments by the Bauhaus artist Josef Albers and also from the work of the painter Victor Vasarely, who had been creating chessboard-like black and white compositions since the mid-1930s. Op Art, especially in its black and white form, dominated graphics, record-cover design, painting and the decorative arts in the mid-1960s, especially in the years 1964 and 1965. The famous Campaign for Nuclear Disarmament (CND) badge, with its black and white geometric design, reflects this; as an image it may be contrasted with the Peace Movement badge of the 1950s, which has a free-flowing design of a dove, inspired by Picasso, on a blue ground. Another familiar black and white 'logo', the

117 Yoko Ono: 'Op Art' photograph on the cover of 'Yoko at Indica', catalogue of an exhibition at the Indica Gallery, London, 1966, a typical example of 1960s black and white design.

'Woolmark' which designates a garment made of new wool, was designed by Francesco Saroglia in 1964.

New exponents of Op Art included the painters Bridget Riley and

118 Josef Albers: *Multiplex A.* Woodcut, 1947. Proto-Op Art from an artist who trained at the Bauhaus.

119 A 1960s badge of the Committee of 100 for Nuclear Disarmament, inspired by Op Art, contrasted with a 1950s Peace Movement badge with a free-form design of a dove, in blue and white, inspired by Picasso.

Jesus Raphael Soto, but the style's influence spread into many other fields. Television was, of course, still black and white, and set designs began to emphasise this heavily. The dress designs of Mary Quant, Ossie Clark, Barbara Hulanicki and Courrèges, and even the heavy black make-up of the period, were all part of this fashion. The Beatles dressed in the style in the mid-1960s. Meanwhile, Vasarely was commissioned to design ceramics for Rosenthal, including the exterior work for their 'Studio Houses'. Vasarely's personal influence was enormous and extended to the art colleges; an example is Neil Harding's black oxidised cylindrical vase, produced in 1965 while he was a student at the Royal College of Art, which has applied sections in the Op style.

Harding's cylinder also reflects the style of the period in its tubular form, sliced off at the top. In general, 1960s design, especially in metal, became more angular and 'cut off'. For example, in the work of the silversmiths Gerald Benney, David Mellor and Robert Welch, mentioned in the last chapter, the Sixties horizontal top edge ousted the

120 Victor Vasarely: Op Art surface decoration of 1978 on a porcelain coffee pot first designed by Ambrogio Pozzi for Rosenthal in 1968.

121 Victor Vasarely: Ceramic
tiles on the façade of the
Rosenthal Studio-Haus in Berlin,
1978.

122 Arne Jacobsen: Stainless
steel 'Cylinda' coffee pot for
Stelton, 1967 – a typical
cylindrical form of the 1960s.

Fifties upswept curve of the lid. A more extreme example is the aptly
named 'Cylinda' line of stainless-steel hollow-ware designed by the
Danish architect Arne Jacobsen in 1967.

Like Harding's vase, Peter Murdoch's 'Spotty' child's chair was
designed while he was a student at the Royal College of Art, but in
1963. Experimental in its use of fibreboard, it, too, is essentially a
folded-in cylinder and the spots give it an Op Art effect.

The 'Mersey sound' poet Adrian Henri captures the spirit of this
period of 'black and white' well in his suite of poems *Pictures from
an Exhibition*, based on paintings shown at the 'Painting and Sculpture
of a Decade' exhibition at the Tate Gallery in 1964. Henri comments
on Albers's *Homage to the square*; and of Jim Dine's *Black Bathroom*
of 1962 he writes:

black splashes on the white walls
interrupting the commercials
TURN ON THE GLEAMING WHITE SINK
AND POEMS COME OUT OF THE TAPS!

Of Vasarely's *Supernovae* of 1959–61 he writes, simply:

Black is White   White is Black

while the poem about Louise Nevelson's painting of 1960 ends:

Black Boxes Black Black Black

It was only a short journey from this style to Minimalism, with its
rectangular emphasis, especially in the 'sculpture' of Don Judd and
Carl André. The latter's famous 'pile of bricks', *Equivalent VIII*,
made in 1966, remade in 1969 and finally acquired by the Tate
Gallery, frightened the philistines, but this kind of statement also
prompted artists to seek more flavour in what some considered to
be the limited diet of formalism.

Pop (popular) Art was one current which introduced a greater
representational ingredient. It was in fact, a child of the 1940s. As
early as 1947, Eduardo Paolozzi had produced a collage, *Intimate Con-
fessions*, which mixed mechanical imagery (gun, US warplane) with
sexual imagery and a Coca-Cola bottle and logo, together with the
word 'Pop'. In that case, the word was treble-coded: the pop of a
gun, pop meaning a fizzy drink and pop for popular. In 1952 Paolozzi
became a member of the Independent Group which gathered at the
Institute of Contemporary Arts in London. Other members included
the writer Lawrence Alloway, the painter Richard Hamilton, the
architects Peter and Alison Smithson and the architectural critic
Reyner Banham. American cars, consumer goods, advertisements, all
excited them. Parodying Marinetti's outburst in the First Futurist
Manifesto of 1909 that 'A racing car . . . is more beautiful than the
Victory of Samothrace', Banham said that a Buick V-8 of 1955 with
its 'glitter . . . bulk . . . and deliberate exposure of technical means'

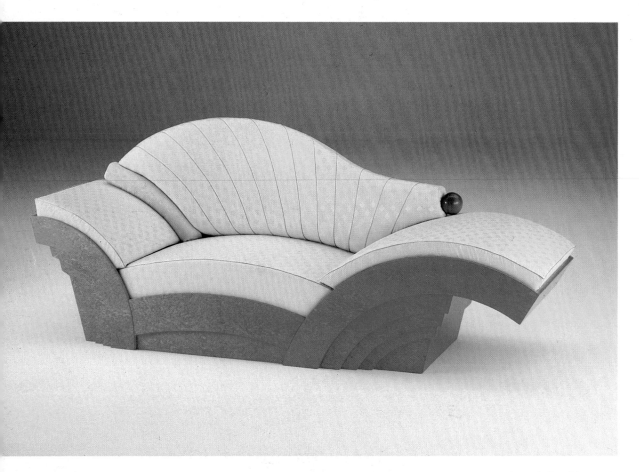

Plate X Hans Hollein: 'Marilyn' sofa in wood and fabric,
for Poltronova, 1981.

Plate XI Paolo Deganello: 'Torso' armchair, with a steel
frame and fabric upholstery, for Cassina, 1982. Deganello
here combines the bright colours of Italian 'new wave'
design with a revival of Fifties free-form shapes.

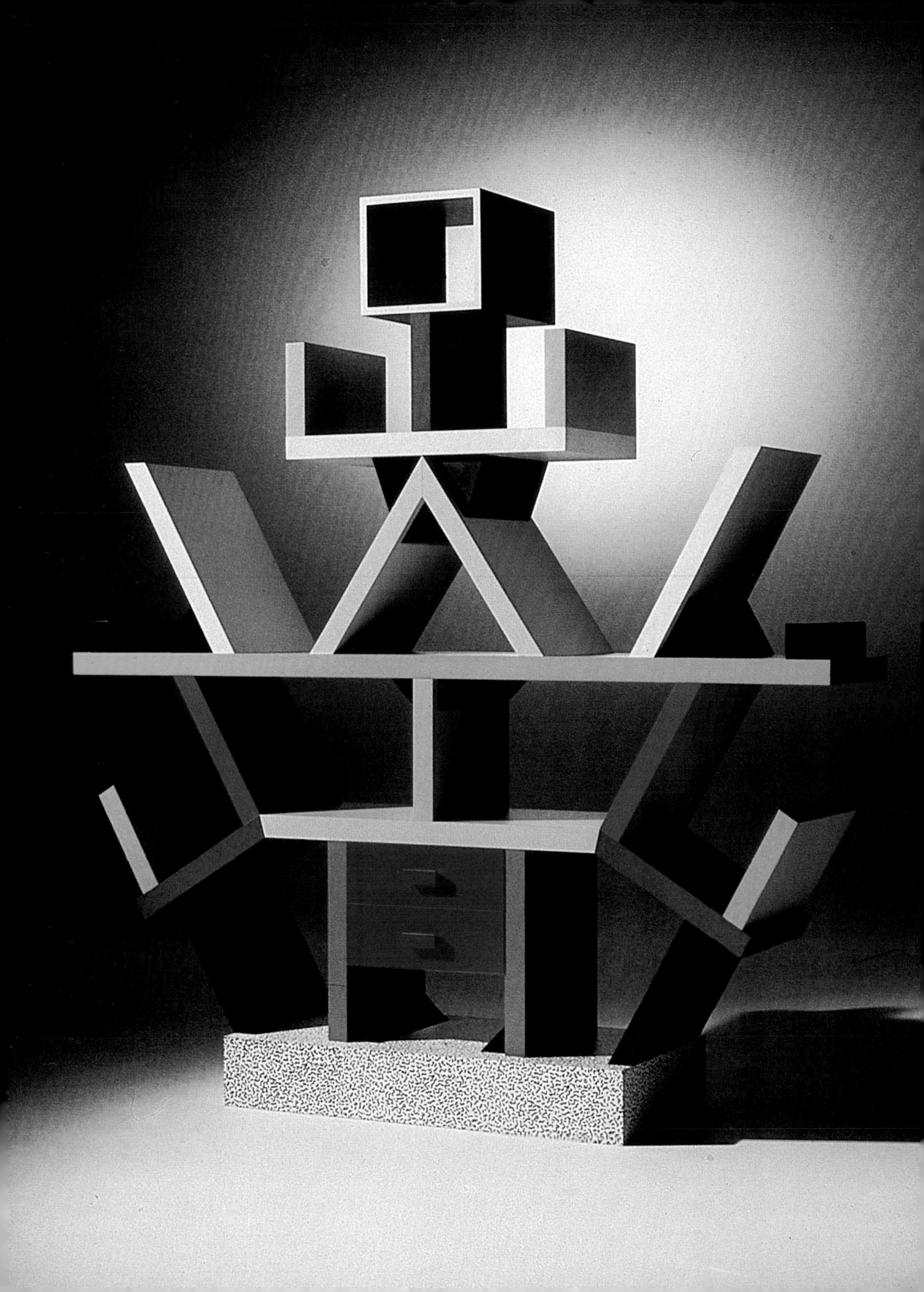

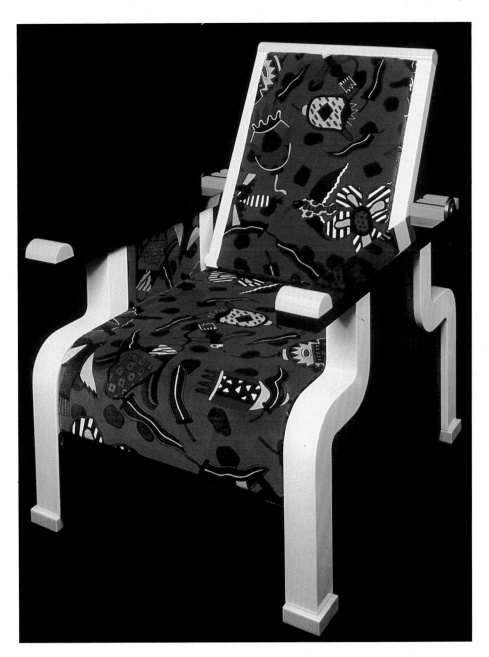

Plate XII *(left)* Ettore Sottsass: 'Carlton'
room divider in plastic laminate, for Memphis,
1981. Italian 'new wave' design is often
distinguished from its cousin, Post-Modern
Classicism, by its use of anthropomorphic or
zoomorphic shapes, and its bright colours.

Plate XIII George Sowden and Nathalie du
Pasquier: 'Mamounia' armchair in lacquered
wood, plastic laminate and velvet, for
Memphis, 1985.

Plate XIV Ettore Sottsass: 'Deneb' glass vase, made by Toso Vetri d'Arte for Memphis, 1982.

Plate XV Ettore Sottsass: 'Alcor' glass vase, made by Toso Vetri d'Arte for Memphis, 1983. Traditional Venetian glass-making processes, with prunts and trailing, are here combined with a fashionable 1950s revival form.

Plate XVI Marco Zanini:
'Colorado' ceramic teapot, made
by Ceramiche Flavia for
Memphis, 1983. Anti-design and
anti-functionalism in baby blues
and pinks.

123 Eduardo Paolozzi:
Automobile Head. Screenprint,
1954. A Pop-Art marriage of car
and robot imagery.

was a more practical design model than the Bauhaus. The Smithsons
said, 'today we collect ads', but the most effective statement was Alloway's, that 'Hollywood, Detroit and Madison Avenue were in terms
of our interests producing the best popular culture', thereby anticipating by some years Tom Wolfe's description of Las Vegas as the
'Versailles of America' or Robert Venturi's fascination with the same
meretricious city, expressed in his book *Learning from Las Vegas*
(1972).

The British Pop artists were sowing seeds through their work as

124 Andy Warhol: *Campbell's Soup*. Screenprint, 1968. A 1960s Pop-Art icon produced from mundane everyday imagery.

125 Richard Hamilton: *The Critic Laughs*. Screenprint, 1968. A 'well-designed' Braun appliance allied to kitsch. The latter became a growing inspiration for designers in the late 1960s.

well as through their statements. Richard Hamilton, shadow-acting the Dadaist interest in sexuality and machinery, produced images of cars and pin-ups in the 1950s; Paolozzi's *Automobile Head* of 1954 was a strange marriage of car and robot imagery. In America, Pop artists, in particular Andy Warhol, began to explore images of consumerism. Warhol's prints, notably his *Campbell's Soup Cans*, used commonplace imagery or repetition to create icons out of everyday

115 · POP AND LIQUORICE ALLSORTS

116 · POP AND LIQUORICE ALLSORTS

126 Eduardo Paolozzi: 'Palladio' surface decoration on a porcelain coffee pot, 'Polygon', designed by Tapio Wirkkala for Rosenthal, 1978.

objects. Richard Hamilton's *The Critic Laughs* of 1968 is on the other hand an almost surreal juxtaposition of good design (the Braun electric toothbrush) and kitsch, or bad taste: a seaside-rock false-teeth palate perches on the Braun base. Hamilton anticipates the next generation's interest in kitsch as well as anti-design in this image, produced in the year during which there was so much unrest in universities, art colleges and politics throughout Europe.

Paolozzi now works not only in printmaking and sculpture but also in ceramics, teaching at the Royal College of Art as well as in Germany. He has designed ceramics for Rosenthal and a witty set of plates for Wedgwood in 1970, as well as mosaics for the London Underground station at Tottenham Court Road (1984). This brightly coloured work is in sharp contrast to the bland caramel-coloured tiles authorised by the 'Medici of the metro', Frank Pick, in the 1930s. Art now supplants design; 1980s colour reduces 'good taste' and in some senses ridicules it. This change made by the Underground reflects a greater public awareness and desire for colour and ornament as a result of the influence of Pop Art, and is symptomatic of a reaction away from purity in design towards ornament in the 'new wave' generation of today.

Post-Modernist design is interwoven with Pop Art developments and represents a reaction against the pure ideas of 'good form' preached by the 1930s architects and patrons. However, this idea of 'good form' has persisted in England as part of the philosophy of the Design Council, which was set up to promote high design standards. It has contributed to the success of Sir Terence Conran, whose Habitat chain of shops emerged in 1964 as an innovator of Bauhaus good form in Great Britain, forty years after its birth in Germany. Le Corbusier's architecture spawned a thousand clones in England, but few of them were conceived as the master would have wished. The high-rise building was not difficult to dislike, and was never better satirised than by Anthony Burgess in his novel *A Clockwork Orange* (1962), where Alex, who speaks 'Nadsat', a teenage argot based in part on Russian, describes his abode thus: 'I lived . . . in Municipal flatblock 18A. I went to the lift, but there was no need to press the electric knopka to see if it was working or not . . . so I had to walk the ten floors up.' Later Alex passes a 'bolshy flatblock called Victoria Flatblock after some victory or other'. Burgess was writing exactly ten years before the event which the influential writer Charles Jencks sees as the death of Modern architecture. In his book *The Language of Post-Modern Architecture* (1977), Jencks writes: 'Happily we can date the death of modern architecture to a precise moment in time. Modern architecture died in St. Louis, Missouri on July 15th 1972.' The event Jencks refers to, the blowing up of the socially undesirable Pruitt-Igoe

high-rise blocks, built only twenty years earlier, is indicative of the widespread antipathy for this type of architecture. The search for a new idiom is understandable from two points of view. First, Modern architecture had made a vital contribution during the period when it was revolutionary, when it held that 'less was more'. Secondly, it had in some ways failed in its main aim, to realise through social engineering a betterment of life. By the mid-1960s and early 1970s it was seen as stale, outworn and unacceptable by a more individualistic generation.

In design as well as in architecture, Pop led the way towards a Post-Modern aesthetic. In England, Archigram – a think-tank of

127 Archizoom: 'Mies' chair and footstool of chromed steel and rubber with pony-skin seat, for Poltronova, 1969. An ironic reference to the great Modern architect-designer Mies van der Rohe, heralding the eclectic historical awareness of Post-Modernism.

young architects who used Pop Art graphics and collage to express fresh thoughts – was formed in 1961. Archigram was the first of three 'A's, the second and third being the groups Archizoom and Alchymia, formed in Italy. Indeed it may well have been an Archigram image of 1964, containing the words 'archigram' and 'zoom', that gave Archizoom its title.

Archizoom was formed in 1966 in Florence, and led by Andrea Branzi, who later worked for both Alchymia and Memphis. He has also written an important survey of what he calls 'new-wave' design, entitled *The Hot House* (1984). At Archizoom, both Branzi and Paolo Deganello, who has more recently produced Fifties free-form revival furniture, became concerned with anti-design and banal design. Their revolutionary approach was typical of the late 1960s, and largely prompted by the political protests of 1968, especially on the streets of Paris and at art colleges throughout Europe. Archizoom's Art Deco revival 'Dream' beds of 1967 and their 'Mies' chair of 1969 swiped at 'good form' and used ironic references to past styles to create modern-day 'art furniture'. Other influences on design in the late 1960s included important books and exhibitions on Art Nouveau and Art Deco, and a revival in the popularity of graphics inspired by the work of Aubrey Beardsley and Alphonse Mucha. Psychedelic art added bizarre colours and tones not dreamed of by the 1890s artists in their wildest hallucinations. Jencks's description of this new Italian work as 'supersensualist' and part of a *dolce-vita* tradition is accurate, but a conscious desire *d'épater le bourgeois* also formed part of the radical ideology of the 1960s generation.

Even in less intellectual Italian circles, Pop Art had an overt influence. The group De Pas, D'Urbino, Lomazzi produced Pop images, like the 'Blow' inflatable chair of 1967. Its form was a witty reference to Eileen Gray's 'Bibendum' chair of 1929, itself referring to the well-known image of the Michelin Man, also known as 'bibendum', used by the company as its logo. Even more 'anti-design' is a chair of 1970 by the same group, called 'Joe' and shaped like an American baseball glove. The reference here is to the baseball hero Joe DiMaggio (former husband of Marilyn Monroe), whose name had featured in Simon and Garfunkel's song 'Mrs Robinson' for Mike Nichols's film *The Graduate* (1967).

The 1970s began to see some definition of 'Post-Modern' architecture, especially in the writings of Charles Jencks, who effectively gave the word 'Post-Modernism' currency even if he did not coin it originally. Jencks's *Modern Movements in Architecture* of 1973 and *The Language of Post-Modern Architecture* of 1977 provide excellent surveys of how, in architecture, anti-rationalism emerged from the work of the Modern architects themselves. The history of Post-

Modern design in the decorative arts, on the other hand, has yet to be written. It clearly shares with architecture a dislike of, or reaction against, the Modern movement, and yet it too has emerged from that movement, with its considerations of 'good form'. Any analysis must include reference to the oldest 'anti-design' renegade, Ettore Sottsass Jr, whose career has been divided between years of 'good form' industrial design for Olivetti and personal anti-design gestures, especially in the 1960s. Sottsass set up his office in Milan in 1946, and throughout the 1950s and 1960s did excellent product design, especially for Olivetti. However, in 1961 he travelled to India, became interested in Pop culture, and around 1965 began to design ceramics for Poltronova inspired in form by Art Deco ziggurats and in title

129 *(right)* De Pas, D'Urbino, Lomazzi: 'E.T.' glass tables for Zanotta, 1983. Aptly named 'E.T.' for Extra-Terrestrial, the feet relate more to Mickey Mouse, a constant design source, and in particular to Sottsass's 'Mickey Mouse' table of 1971.

128 Ettore Sottsass: Ceramic vases, 'Il Sostante' and 'Il Sestante', with Op Art decoration, for Poltronova, about 1965.

by Indian mysticism, for example his 'Tantra' vase. Sottsass became part of Studio Alchymia, the Milanese 'group' formed in 1979 by Alessandro Mendini, who became editor of *Domus* on the death of Gio Ponti. Alchymia's work, and especially that of Mendini, contains much 'banal design', such as his 'Proust' chair of 1978, decorated in the divisionist style of Seurat, or his second-hand furniture of the same year painted in the style and colours of Kandinsky. Mendini's work is characteristic of an age of eclecticism which permits this type of gesture. It is significant that Branzi, the 'anti-designer' of the 1960s, also worked with Alchymia.

It was not long, however, before Sottsass, the elder statesman of Italian design, seceded from Alchymia to form his own group, Memphis, surrounding himself with designers who were almost all under thirty. The group was started in 1981. The reason for the choice of the name Memphis is enigmatic, but it was apparently inspired by Bob Dylan's record 'Stuck inside of Mobile with the Memphis Blues Again' (1966), which was played over and over again at a gathering of the group. Curiously, the song may also have suggested the title of William Tucker's brightly coloured sculpture *Memphis* (1966; now in the Tate Gallery, London). Even as the name of a city, Memphis is ambiguous, referring both to Memphis, Tennessee, and to the ancient Egyptian city of culture. Nothing could be more appropriate as a title for a Post-Modern style than a blend of Pop and ancient culture, for, as we shall see, a revival of classicism is yet another column in the edifice of Post-Modern design.

In a confused age when a sense of history and popular culture meet, Memphis can perhaps be described as the ultimate 'fruit salad'. The culinary image is not misplaced in an appreciation of the 'style'. Branzi, who has worked for the group, illustrates his own hotly coloured photograph of liquorice allsorts, taken in 1976, in his book *The Hot House*; the title of the book is a good image, a metaphor for growth. Sottsass has said: 'Anything that is tamed by culture loses its flavour after a while, it's like eating cardboard. You have to put mustard on it or take little pieces of cardboard and eat them with tomatoes and salad. It's a lot better if you don't eat cardboard at all.' Memphis objects seem to be almost edible, painted in food colours, with references to cassata and tutti-frutti. Nathalie du Pasquier's fabrics have even been compared to sweet wrappers.

Memphis represents many different viewpoints under the umbrella of one name. The work of Michele de Lucchi is the most lucid: like Sottsass, he was a member of Alchymia, and at that stage, in 1979, he rethought product-design appliances such as fans, vacuum cleaners and irons, which he painted in baby blues, powder pinks and yellows. His Memphis work is usually symmetrical, with much use of 'Op

130 Matteo Thun: 'Chad' ceramic teapot, made by Porcellane San Marco for Memphis, 1982 – a humorous hybrid between a toy tank and a duck. Thun is emerging as one of the most adventurous ceramic designers of the 1980s.

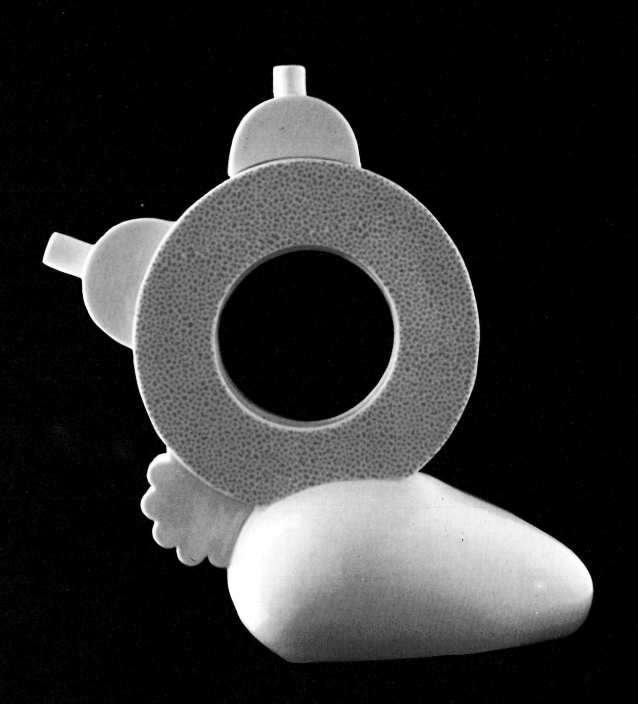

131 Ettore Sottsass: 'Hyatt'
table in briar-wood and metal, for
Memphis, 1984. An example of
Sottsass's more 'classical' work.

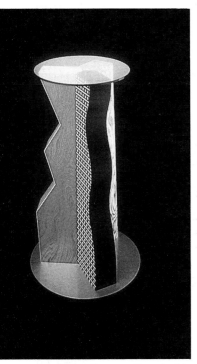

132 Ettore Sottsass: 'Ivory' table
in wood veneer, plastic laminate
and glass, for Memphis, 1985. A
highly 'sculptural' design which
perhaps suggests Picasso's
synthetic Cubism as a source.

Art' black and white, contrasted with hot and cold colours. De Lucchi
has claimed that he was inspired in London on New Year's Eve 1980
by Punks and their bizarre make-up. However, he has also been
influenced by the Fifties revival, since working on a 1950s exhibition
in Milan in 1977. An example of this tendency is his 'First' chair,
with its blue circular backrest and balls for armrests.

Kitsch or 'bad taste' began to be taken seriously again, especially
in Italy, after the publication of essays on the subject by Gillo Dorfles
in 1969. Sottsass began to use 'suburban' materials, such as laminates
and plastic. Nearly all the Memphis group use coloured laminates
which imitate marble, *faux* surfaces which would make an Arts and
Crafts 'moral' designer turn in his grave. Other influences include
colours based on third-world flags and textiles – these have particularly inspired Nathalie du Pasquier's fabrics – and everything from
Hollywood Deco through to Fifties asymmetrical furniture. Even
1930s rationalism has been revived in Andrea Branzi's work. References to specifically Italian materials, such as mosaic and marble, are
particularly frequent, while in glass a long Venetian tradition can be
detected behind the designs of Sottsass and Marco Zanini. Sottsass's
work in this medium is exciting: his asymmetrical 'Sol' fruit dish of
blown glass, produced by Toso Vetri D'Arte, Murano, has a Fifties
feel to it, while his 'Alioth' and 'Alcor' vases of 1983 are interesting
blends of the form of the industrial electrical isolator with 'traditional'
Venetian types of decoration, coloured trailing and assertive prunts.
The concertina form of porcelain isolator lies behind some of Marco
Zanini's ceramics, especially 'Victoria' of 1983, which is topped with
an ice-cream-like confection of cockscomb form which might almost
have been taken out of context from a Kandinsky painting. The cockscomb is a typical Memphis motif.

One of the most gifted young designers attached to Memphis is
Matteo Thun, whose ceramics echo Sottsass's interest in anthropomorphic and zoomorphic forms. Sottsass's 'Carlton' room divider in
plastic laminate (1981) has as its central feature the stylised shape
of a man: Thun's ceramics are strutting birds. One of the best of
these, a geometric form in grey, pink and mauve, is aptly called 'Peli-
canus Bellicosus' (1982). The Hamburg-born couturier Karl Lager-
feld has an apartment in Monte Carlo filled with Thun's best creations
and a bedside lamp designed by Sottsass resembling a nodding bird.
No 'cardboard' is eaten in this apartment!

Sottsass's *ennui* with good form is expressed through the energy
of a generation of young designers who are post-Pop; Michele de Lucchi and Nathalie du Pasquier were born only in 1951 and 1957
respectively.

We have already seen that design and sculpture have sometimes

125 · POP AND LIQUORICE ALLSORTS

been strongly linked, especially in the 1950s. Memphis responds, to some extent, to all the visual arts: architecture, painting, sculpture, ceramics, glass, metalwork and furniture are blended to create a new way of looking. Sottsass's more recent work, for example his glass-topped side table of 1985 called 'Ivory', crosses the boundary between sculpture and design, in much the same way that Picasso bridged the gap between painting and sculpture during his synthetic Cubist period of 1912–14.

It is significant, finally, that Memphis has embraced the work of two members of the 'Post-Modern Classical' style, the American Michael Graves and the Austrian Hans Hollein. In *Complexity and Contradiction in Architecture* Venturi countered the International Modern movement's credo of 'less is more' with the now famous statement 'less is a bore', and Post-Modern Classicism is as unnervingly catholic as Post-Modernism itself. Despite Venturi's appeal in that same book for 'elements which are hybrid rather than pure . . . messy vitality over obvious unity', other designers have searched for a valid understanding of order, and by extension, the classical 'orders'.

133 Robert Venturi: Chestnut Hill House, Pennsylvania, 1963. One of the first Post-Modern buildings, designed by Venturi for his mother. The split gable is loosely based on a similar form at Blenheim Palace, designed by Vanbrugh and Hawksmoor in the early eighteenth century.

The new classicism is tinged with political overtones, as the neo-classicism of the 1930s has always been seen by most 'Moderns' as the style of totalitarianism and not that of the ideal social order. It has been embraced especially by critics of the new right in England who actually form part of a rearguard which believes that 1930s Modern was an aberration, to be erased forever. Others eagerly accept classicism for the sake of conservation, and equate Modern architecture with urbanisation and destruction. For Americans, on the other hand, it might be logical to see classicism as their natural style, as it was prevailing at the time of the birth of the American nation in 1776. Germans might see it as part of an uninterrupted tradition stretching from the ideas of the Enlightenment thinkers Lessing,

134 Ian Hamilton Finlay: 'Virtue' and 'Terror' medal, 1983. An ironic Post-Modernist reference to neo-classicism, playing on the idea of the 'reverse side of the coin'.

Winckelmann and Goethe to the architecture of Schinkel and Semper. Even the great Austrian and German 'Moderns', Adolf Loos, Peter Behrens and Ludwig Mies van der Rohe, revived 'classicism' and 'neo-classicism' in their architecture. As early as 1910, Adolf Loos said of Schinkel: 'We have forgotten him. May the light of this towering figure shine upon our forthcoming generation of architects.'

It is therefore not surprising that on the lips and no doubt in the libraries of Post-Modern architects are the works of the lions of the eighteenth century, Sir John Soane and K.F. Schinkel, and the paper tigers Etienne-Louis Boullée and Claude Nicolas Ledoux, whose details are easy to quote. Some Post-Modernist architects are slowly relearning the classical tradition and are becoming more aware of the longer history of architecture and design which was consciously rejected by the preceding generation. And the life-support is of course the column, any column, however it may relate to the classical orders. In 1983, the Scottish artist Ian Hamilton Finlay, whose work expresses a profound interest in the classical tradition, defined neo-classicism in his *An Illustrated Dictionary of the Little Spartan War*

as a 'rearmament programme for architecture and the arts'. If this
is so, then the column is the major weapon.

This love of columns extends to Pop culture and the bright colours
of Italian design. As early as the mid-1970s, Gufram in Italy produced
a moulded foam chair called 'Capitello', in the shape of an Ionic
capital. In 1980 the Swiss architect Robert Haussmann designed a
fluted column drawer unit in lacquered wood for Studio Alchymia,
called 'Colonna'. At the same time, and fundamentally more seriously,
Ian Hamilton Finlay has erected obelisks, columns and witty tributes
to classical script incised in stone, in his house and garden at
Stonypath. Finlay's artistic interests parallel those of many architects
and range from the French Revolution to the Third Reich.

In his survey *Post-Modern Classicism*, published in 1980, Charles
Jencks has chosen to include his own work as well as that of the Americans Robert Venturi, Charles Moore, Michael Graves and Robert
Stern, the Italian Aldo Rossi, the Austrian Hans Hollein and the
Englishman James Stirling. The American architect Philip Johnson
has also been converted to classicism. His controversial A.T. & T.
skyscraper building in New York of 1979–83 has a broken pediment
top and its base is a stripped Roman triumphal arch. Meanwhile, other

135 Studio 65: 'Capitello'
moulded foam chair, for Gufram,
1971. An Ionic capital translated
into furniture. Post-Modern
Classical design has its origins in
pieces like this.

136 Philip Johnson: A.T. & T. skyscraper, New York, 1978–83. This building marks Johnson's conversion from Modernism to Post-Modernism. The base is a classical triumphal arch, and the top is 'Chippendale'. Next to it is the IBM building.

architects in England, notably Quinlan Terry, continue a tradition of purer neo-classicism.

It is only very recently that Post-Modernist architects have ventured into the area of 'design', and their excursions into the decorative arts have been exciting. In 1979 the Italian metalwork company Alessi invited eleven architects to design a silver tea or coffee service. The commission was unusual in that Alessi normally produces stainless steel. The result, as we shall see, brought together Post-Modern and Post-Modern Classical design. Then in 1982, Formica held a 'surface and ornament design' competition for 'Colorcore', a new version of their plastic laminate, for which Venturi and Moore, among others, designed interesting 'furniture'.

Before an analysis can be made of the individual contributions of the designers, it is important to stress how far the pluralism of the 1980s allows for tributes to other periods. Since the war, the growth in design awareness has been phenomenal, marked by publications on almost all the major figures of the nineteenth and early twentieth centuries. Since the 1960s there has been admiration for both Gaudí and Mackintosh; both are mentioned in the 'Mersey-sound' poem 'Me – if you weren't you, who would you like to be?' by Adrian Henri

(1967). Like that of Mackintosh, the work of Josef Hoffmann and the Wiener Werkstätte has been extensively published, studied and reproduced. The significance of Hoffmann for Post-Modernism lies in his ability to be multi-faceted. His use of classical quotation and 'fluting' in his metalwork and glass is now admired, just as his 'decadent' later phase of the 1920s, with its rococo undertones, has been in recent years. In the late 1970s, at a time of interest in 'high-tech' design and industrial grid patterning in furnishings, it was his 'square' metalwork which was in vogue. Hoffmann surely is the 'man for all seasons' and will no doubt continue to enjoy posthumous sway over Post-Modernists. The theoretical writings and architecture of Adolf Loos, especially his rediscovered classicism, have also had a strong influence, and no doubt the eccentric, ambidextrous work of Christopher Dresser has its Post-Modern following. In the 1930s, these men were seen, especially by Nikolaus Pevsner, as pioneers of Modern design, as if they were all working in a determinist way towards an ideal of modernity. Now, in the eclectic Eighties, they may also be seen as pioneers of Post-Modernism: Mackintosh for his colour and ornament; Hoffmann for his classicism and his 'decadent' *Gemütlichkeit* of the Twenties; Gaudí for his eccentricity and anti-rationalism, and Dresser for his use of ornament rather than his functionalism. Many of these designers, when looked at carefully, are seen to conform to Venturi's demands for 'messy vitality over obvious unity'.

Venturi himself designed a coffee service for Alessi, commissioned in 1979 and completed in 1983, which reflects the complexity of our age. Its rounded form could broadly be called 'Georgian' in spirit, and yet its surface decoration of tea-leaves pays homage to the conventionalised patterns of the Wiener Werkstätte. The leaf metaphor even goes back to Henry Cole's Summerly group with its interest in appropriate decoration. For the Colorcore 'surface and ornament' competition in 1982, Venturi produced a 'mirror in the Greek revival manner' with classical fluted decoration, and yet one can point to the existence of similar frames in the early 1900s; one such hung in the studio of Dr Hugo Henneberg, an Austrian patron of both Hoffmann and Mackintosh. What makes Venturi's mirror specifically Post-Modern is that it is *plastic* classic. Venturi's most extreme contribution to Post-Modern design, given the history of Knoll as a producer of good Modern furniture, is the set of chairs he designed for them in 1984. Laminated, some with bizarre Memphis-like colours, these chairs were designed in nine styles, ranging from 'Queen Anne' to 'Art Deco' via 'Chippendale' and 'Empire', but only the fretted backs make witty reference to each epoch as it is remembered. A reincarnated George Washington would fail to recognise them as

137 Robert Venturi: 'Queen Anne' table and four chairs in the 'Grandmother' pattern, for Knoll International, 1984. Venturi has designed chairs in nine styles, ranging from 'Queen Anne' to 'Art Deco'. His tea service for Alessi, designed between 1979 and 1983, can be seen on the table.

accurate versions of the eighteenth-century styles, and Chippendale would disown them, just as he would the so-called 'Chippendale' top of Johnson's A.T. & T. skyscraper.

Michael Graves, architect of the controversial Post-Modern Classical Public Services' Building, Portland, Oregon (1982), designed furniture for Sunar between 1979 and 1981, as well as their showroom in New York. His tables have fluted pedestals and false marble surfaces. Perhaps his most successful work has been for Memphis, notably his highly 'architectural' 'Plaza' dressing table of 1981 and

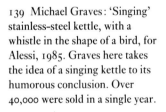

138 Michael Graves: 'Plaza' dressing table in maple-root wood and mirror glass, for Memphis, 1981. A Hollywood revival fantasy and an example of 'architectural' design.

'Stanhope' bed of 1982. They differ from much other Memphis work in being of maple-root wood, which gives them an Art Deco as well as a neo-classical feel (Sottsass, too, has begun very recently to use this classical wood look). The dressing table is a 'Hollywood' fantasy with Art Deco-style mirror-glass tesserae. The use of this 'blond wood' effect reinforces the connection that the Post-Modernists see between furniture of the 1930s and the 1830s, where Deco meets Empire. Likewise, Graves's 1983 silver coffee service for Alessi is full of witty art-historical references: neo-classical fluting in metal, with just a hint of Hoffmann's interpretation of the same theme in his Wiener Werkstätte productions of the 1920s.

As might be expected, Charles Jencks's recent excursions into design have produced a witty hybrid of classicism and Art Deco. His 'Sun' chairs, which echo Regency and Deco 'sunbursts' in their decorative motifs, are again a fashionable compression of 1930 and 1830. His silver service for Alessi is a tribute to volutes, fluting, rams' heads and the broken column. The whole is 'look at me how clever' but at the same time an extraordinary betrayal of every lesson in functionalism and ergonomics learned since the days of Christopher Dresser.

It is interesting that the work of another American architect, Richard Meier, for Alessi has resulted in a Post-Modernist 'Modern revival' piece, in fact a direct homage to Kasimir Malevich. Meier's

139 Michael Graves: 'Singing' stainless-steel kettle, with a whistle in the shape of a bird, for Alessi, 1985. Graves here takes the idea of a singing kettle to its humorous conclusion. Over 40,000 were sold in a single year.

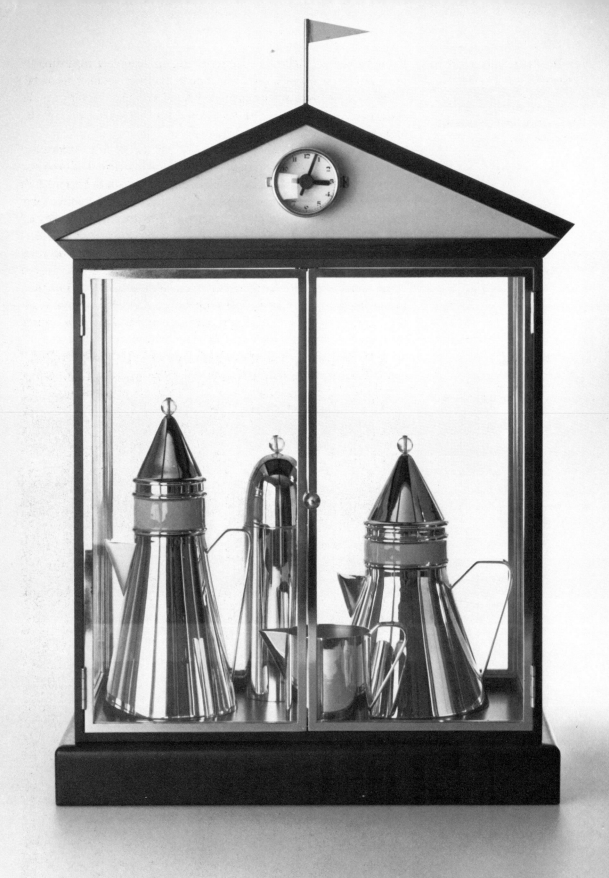

140 Aldo Rossi: Silver service in a pedimented case, for Alessi, 1981. Design as 'micro-architecture': the whole refers to Rossi's design for the Teatro del Mondo (fig. 141).

silver set echoes Malevich's famous porcelain teapot of 1923 directly and cleverly, as we see the idea 'translated' from ceramic to metal. Meier's other silver-plate designs for Swid Powell in America make references to Hoffmann and Kolo Moser in their '*quadratl*' phases, and are pierced accordingly.

Three Italians, Aldo Rossi, Paolo Portoghesi and Alessandro Mendini, also produced designs for Alessi's competition. These run the gamut of Post-Modernism from Rossi's classicism to Portoghesi's Hoffmannisms and Mendini's 'banal' humour. Rossi's coffee pots refer to his own Post-Modern architectural designs, and his set nestles in a pedimented case. The whole ensemble is reminiscent of his exciting design for the Teatro del Mondo, a floating theatre made of wood and steel for Venice in 1979. The coffee pots refer to this theatre and at the same time gently plagiarise the form of the top of the Campanile in St Mark's Square. Portoghesi's coffee service for Alessi has a Viennese feel, but the decorative band of black and white enamel refers

141 Aldo Rossi: Teatro del Mondo, Venice, 1979. A Post-Modern floating theatre of wood and steel, designed for the 1980 Venice Biennale.

142 Aldo Rossi: 'La Conica' stainless-steel espresso coffee-makers, for Alessi, 1984. Like the silver service shown in fig. 140, this design refers to Rossi's Teatro del Mondo, and in turn to the Campanile in St Mark's Square, Venice.

to Op Art as well as to the Wiener Werkstätte. (Portoghesi is joint author of a book on Viennese decorative art, *La Seggiola di Vienna*, published in 1976.) The black and white effects in Viennese work have influenced much Italian design, and it is interesting that in 1985 Alessandro Mendini designed an 'Op Art' black and white surface decoration for the Renault 5 car. Mendini's silver set for Alessi makes use of a basic egg-cup shape on a single pedestal base, with echoes of Wiener Werkstätte metalwork, though the whole has a bird-like quality and reminds one of a flamingo, a feature shared with some of the Memphis ceramics of Matteo Thun.

Richard Sapper, a German-born designer who has worked extensively in Italy and was responsible for some of the best serious lighting product design in the 1970s, has also caught on to the 'fun' of Post-Modern design with his 'Bollitore' kettle for Alessi. This kettle combines a traditional 'good form' dome-shaped body with a whistle in the shape of the dangerous end of a Wild West six-shooter. The handle has the form of a cockscomb, reminiscent of Memphis work but also intelligently indented for greater purchase in the hand; when boiling, the kettle emits the sound of an American steam locomotive. The gun reference seems to have returned full circle to the British origins of Pop; one is reminded of Eduardo Paolozzi's collage of 1947 with its revolver.

143 Matteo Thun: 'Nefertiti'
ceramic tea-set, made by
Ceramiche Flavia for Memphis,
1981.

144 Richard Sapper: 'Bollitore'
stainless-steel kettle for Alessi,
1983. When boiling, the kettle
produces the sound of an
American steam locomotive
(pitched notes 'E' and 'B').

145 Hans Hollein: Austrian
Travel Bureau, Vienna, 1978.
Hollein here draws upon the
architecture of Otto Wagner, and
the palm-tree columns refer to a
similar idiom used by Nash in the
Brighton Pavilion.

The 1983 Alessi competition also attracted a Spanish architect, the
Barcelona-born Oscar Tusquets. His tea service, which refers strongly
to shell shapes, goes back to a ground-norm of nature for inspiration
as well as to Gaudí's brilliant curvilinear work from the turn of this
century.

The most gifted of all Post-Modernist architects and designers may
well prove to be the Austrian Hans Hollein, who graduated in America
in 1960. His dual Austro-American background has been very influential: he has absorbed the lessons of Adolf Loos in his architecture,
and perhaps also some of his élitism – his admission that 'architecture
is an affair of the élite' coincided with the emergence of the self-
concerned and personally ambitious 'me' generation. The luxurious
marble of Hollein's façade for the Schullin jewellery shop in Vienna
(1975) echoes the marble shop fronts executed by Loos, especially
in the Kärntner Strasse in the same city, in the first decade of this
century. Hollein even 'quoted' Loos directly in his façade for La
Strada Novissima, the Post-Modern fantasy street display in Venice
directed by Paolo Portoghesi in 1980: one of the columns was a copy
of Loos's unrealised Doric Chicago Tribune Column of 1922. It is
ironic that in 1923 Loos prophesied: 'the great Greek Doric column
will be built. If not in Chicago then in another city. If not for the
Chicago Tribune, then for someone else. If not by me, then by another
architect.' Again, in his Austrian Travel Bureau in Vienna of 1976–8,
Hollein 'quoted' the glass roof of Otto Wagner's famous Viennese
Post Office Savings Bank of 1906; inside, a fluted column is broken
half-way up to reveal a shiny metallic core. Hollein thus combines
classicism and modern technology, in a way that is highly appropriate
for a travel bureau, aiming to suggest escape to another world through
modern technology. (An analogy would be an Air-India jet with ogee-
shaped windows.)

Hollein's interest in the decorative arts has also produced excellent
results. He shares with Ian Hamilton Finlay a fascination with classicism and, uncannily, with aircraft carriers. In 1964 Hollein produced
a surreal photomontage of 'an aircraft carrier in the Austrian wheat-
fields': the image becomes even more bizarre when one remembers
that Austria is totally land-locked. In 1983, Hollein repeated the aircraft carrier image for Alessi, and his silver set for the competition
nestles neatly in position on its carrier-shaped tray, ready to 'take
off' in the user's hands. The pun on 'carrier' is reminiscent of 1970s
conceptual art, especially Simon Cutts's *Aircraft carrier bag*, a screenprint on an actual paper bag, of 1972. Of all the Alessi submissions,
Hollein's work shows the greatest genius and originality.

Hollein has also designed a remarkable piece of furniture for Memphis, his 'Schwarzenberg' table of 1981 in briar-wood, which, like

Graves's work for Memphis, has a Deco-classical 'bleached wood' look. It is shallow-stepped, an inversion of the ziggurat form, and again one is reminded of Loos's interest in a step-pyramid method of 'stacking' roof lines. Wittier still, and an *embarras de richesses* of sources, is Hollein's aptly named 'Marilyn' sofa for Poltronova in Italy (1985). It is a Hollywood casting couch, a Deco screen goddess couch and a neo-classical couch all in one. Its name refers to one of the best-known Pop kitsch seats designed by Studio 65 for Gufram in the 1960s, shaped like lips, coloured red, and also called 'Marilyn'. A Sixties tribute to Marilyn Monroe, this was itself an update of the original 'Mae West's Lips' sofa made in 1937 for Edward James by Jean Michel Franck to Salvador Dali's design. The whole idea goes back ultimately to Dali's gouache *The Face of Mae West* (1935).

The complicated signals sent out by such a couch are part of the 'dragnet' approach of Post-Modernism. Here Hollein's vocabulary draws upon classicism, screen Deco, Surrealism, sexuality, Pop and

146 Hans Hollein: 'Aircraft carrier' silver tea and coffee service, for Alessi, 1983.

kitsch in one fell swoop, while raising a smile: he has certainly satisfied Venturi's demand for 'elements which are hybrid rather than pure'.

Hollein's work brings us face to face with the fundamental question put by Hal Foster in his preface to *Postmodern Culture*, a collection of essays published in 1983: 'Postmodernism: does it exist at all, and if so, what does it mean? Is it a concept or a practice, a matter of local style, or a whole new period or economic phase? What are its

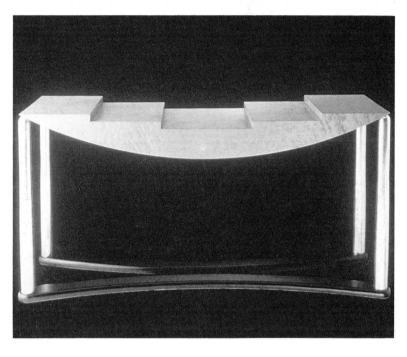

147 Hans Hollein: 'Schwarzenberg' table in briar-wood, for Memphis, 1981. Hollein here combines Post-Modern Classical austerity with a Deco-classical blond wood look.

forms, effects, place? How are we to mark its advent? Are we truly beyond the modern, truly in (say) a post industrial age?'

In design, or so it seems, Post-Modernism is almost anything which is not a tribute to the 'heroic period' of Modern architecture and design between the wars. This raises the issue of how far we can have, say, a Post-Modern car or aeroplane, to which the answer must be that, apart from surface decoration, we cannot. We may be in a post-industrial society, yet all our industrial artefacts reflect an evolving technology. Post-Modernism is in the main a post-Pop Art manifestation. Its 'art content' is unlikely to have much influence on the design of, say, a micro-chip or a tractor. And since it uses modern materials, such as plastic or laminates, Post-Modernism is essentially extending Modernism, not denying its technical achievements. In its 'snakes and ladders' attitude to art and design history (back to the Thirties, the Fifties, up to science fiction, punk, suburbia) it is clearly playing a game.

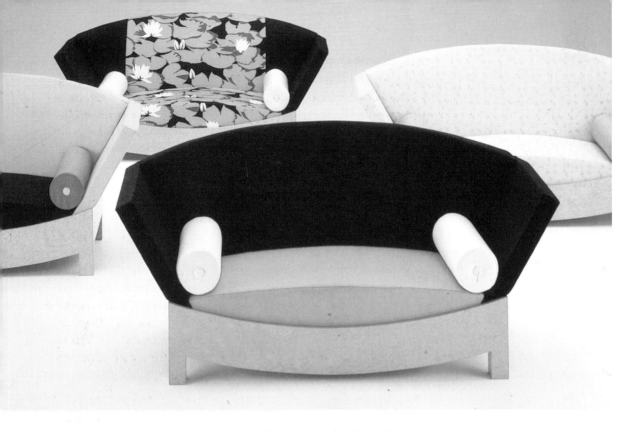

It may well be that Post-Modern Classicism, on the other hand, is a serious attempt to counter the sheer hedonism of the movement it finds itself a part of. Beyond the visual imperialism of classicism, at a time of the decline and fall of perhaps the whole Western Empire, it reintroduces a set of rules to counter the anarchy of the Eighties. The current interest in the eighteenth-century cityscape is reflected, for example, in Sir John Summerson's *The Architecture of the Eighteenth Century* (1986). Post-Modern Classicism also recognises theoretically based socially conscious ideas. Nowhere is this more evident than in the work of the Krier brothers, Robert and Leon. The latter, especially, has been involved with neo-classical reconstruction schemes for Washington DC and Berlin, almost echoing Loos's cry from the wilderness at the start of this century that 'at the beginning of the nineteenth century we departed from tradition. That is the point from which I want to continue.' Especially in his writings in *Art and Design* magazine, Krier has shown his concern with social and urban issues, and this separates him and other 'classicists' from the 'me' gestures of Post-Modernism.

What is also apparent is a movement in fine art towards a redefinition of classicism or classical values. Even Andy Warhol, whose work in the 1960s was quintessentially Pop Art, moved in that direction: examples are his acrylic and silkscreen on canvas images of 1982, such

148 Hans Hollein: 'Mitzi' sofa in wood and fabric, for Poltronova, 1981.

as *Monument for 16 soldiers* and *Friedrich Monument* which echo the quiet, noble grandeur of neo-classicism and its reinterpretation during the Nazi period. 'New realism' in all its forms includes a return to figurative painting. Its most extreme exponents are, perhaps inevitably, Italians, who have a clear understanding of the classicism in the art, say, of Giorgio de Chirico between 1914 and 1918 and in Italian design under Mussolini. This legacy is demonstrated especially clearly in the hard-edged 'neo-classical' revivalism of Carlo Maria Mariani, with its pastiche of the 'erotic frigidaire' style of painting. Even the work of young students in British design colleges, at their degree shows in the summer of 1986, displays a revived interest in the forms of classicism.

It is too early to predict the course of events during the next few years, and it is perhaps sufficient to end this survey with three quotations, which refer to the beginning, middle and latter years of this century. The first is a reminiscence by Loos's last wife, Elsie Altmann, taken from her book *Adolf Loos, der Mensch*, published in Vienna in 1968, and describes his early interest in chairs from antiquity, particularly Egypt:

> Loos admired the chairs in the British Museum, ordered copies
> of the chairs, and had them brought to Vienna, where old Veillich,
> his furniture maker, was to copy them for years to come.

The second quotation was written in 1938, in the heyday of the Modern movement, by Alfred Barr of the Museum of Modern Art, New York:

> Others of us, in architectural Schools, were beginning our courses
> with gigantic renderings of Doric capitals . . . It is no wonder then
> that young Americans began to turn their eyes towards the
> Bauhaus as the one school in the world where modern problems
> of design were approached realistically in a modern atmosphere.

Finally, an 'artwork' made in 1981 by Ian Hamilton Finlay (Claude Chimérique is a fictitious character, and presumably an invented *alterego* of Finlay, bearing a name that suggests the French Revolution):

> 'In the back of every dying civilisation
> sticks a bloody Doric column.'
>
>   Herbert Read, quoted by Charles Jencks
>
> 'In the foreground of every revolution
> invisible, it seems, to the academics,
> stands a perfect classical column.'
>
>   Claude Chimérique, quoted by Ian Hamilton Finlay

CONCLUSION

T he debate between Post-Modern and later Modern 'high-tech' design and architecture will doubtless continue over the next few decades, and indeed it shows every sign of sharpening into a style war. In 1977, for example, Charles Jencks cited Berthold Lubetkin's Highpoint II flats of 1938, with their Greek caryatids, as a precursor of Post-Modern Classicism, and yet, speaking in 1982, Lubetkin described Post-Modernism as 'transvestite architecture, Hepplewhite and Chippendale in drag'. Again, in 1986 Jencks praised James Stirling's Neue Staatsgalerie in Stuttgart as 'the most "real" beauty of post-modern architecture to date' though the architect himself wrote in 1981 'I don't think that our work attempts to be post-modernist'. Indeed, Stirling calls some parts of his gallery (which also makes neo-classical and neo-International Modern references) 'high-tech'.

The Modern movement has demonstrated its capacity to modify its aims and to progress, and it could be argued that it is only now that the high degree of technology it requires has become available, in marked contrast to the crude technology of the 1920s. Two of high-tech's greatest exponents, Richard Rogers and Norman Foster, have shown in their recent buildings, respectively Lloyd's of London and the headquarters of the Hongkong and Shanghai Banking Corporation, both completed in 1986, that the tradition of modern engineering going back to the Crystal Palace of 1851 is far from dead; Paxton's great structure is 'quoted' by both of them. It is significant that both Rogers and Stirling visited, in 1959, the seminal and prophetic Modern precursor of high-tech, the Maison de Verre in Paris of 1928–32, by Pierre Chareau; Rogers's work also realises some of the visionary aspects of Russian Constructivist architecture. It is true that these three architects have concentrated on building rather than on small-scale artefacts or furniture; but in this context it is interesting to note that many designs, especially of furniture, from the 'heroic' period of Modern architecture are still being manufactured, including Hans Coray's proto-high-tech masterpiece of 1939, an aluminium chair with

circular holes in its seat. This chair was even 'quoted' by the British high-tech designer Rodney Kinsman in his own design for his 'Omstak' chair of 1971. In 1978, Joan Kron and Suzanne Slesin wrote *High Tech – the industrial style and source book for the home* and although what they illustrated, for example industrial rubber flooring and Meccano-like shelving, is less in evidence in the home of the 1980s, high-tech is still very much part of architecture.

Critics have often attempted to bury movements alive; Jencks began with Modernism in the 1970s, and now Deyan Sudjic has written in 1986 that Post-Modernism is 'a short term diversion, like art nouveau perhaps, rather than a long-lasting affair'. Early this century, the British art-historian Roger Fry coined the term 'Post-Impressionism' for a style that emerged from Impressionism and yet was in some ways a reaction against it. The same may be said of Post-Modernism, save that the label has been applied while the movement is still in its infancy. Post-Impressionism and Impressionism continued to co-exist side by side, and this is also true of Post-Modernism and the Modern movement, which remind one of Samuel Beckett's two tramps, held together in time, perhaps forever awaiting their Godot.

In 1938, the year in which Alfred Barr damned the Doric column in the comment quoted at the end of the last chapter, the architectural cartoonist Osbert Lancaster wrote his satirical history *Pillar to Post*. Were he alive today, he might reverse the title and call it 'Post to Pillar'. On the Post-Modern side, Hans Hollein and Robert Venturi, for example, have worked with increasing vision, but the same must also be said for the Late Modern camp which includes Richard Rogers and Norman Foster. The design world continues to shadow-act these developments in architecture. Will the pluralism of the 1980s perhaps continue into the second millennium, with 'style wars' between the Post-Modern pedestals and porticos and the high-tech aluminium atriums and titanium towers of the year 2000?

149 Richard Rogers: Lloyd's of London, 1986.

A-Z OF ARTISTS AND DESIGNERS

AALTO, Alvar (1898–1976)

Finnish architect and designer. Aalto studied architecture at the Polytechnic in Helsinki from 1918 to 1921. He established himself as an architect in 1923, and his Sanatorium at Paimio (1929–33) is a classic of International Modern architecture. At the same time he began to design plywood chairs, and in 1935 set up a firm, Artek, to market his simple and successful furniture. Some of his plywood is cantilevered like Bauhaus tubular steel, but clearly softer in finish. His furniture was successful in England and in America and prompted other experiments in that direction, notably by Jack *Pritchard*. From 1937 he designed glass for Iittala, using asymmetrical shapes and subtle curves. Though part of the International Modern movement, Aalto was always sensitive to brick as a material, and he was one of the gentler exponents of Modern forms.

ASHBEE, Charles Robert (1863–1942)

British architect and designer. Ashbee studied history at King's College, Cambridge, and was apprenticed to the architect G.F. Bodley from 1883 to 1885. Inspired by the writing of *Ruskin*, he lived and worked at the philanthropic foundation Toynbee Hall in London's East End. He met *Morris* in 1887, and founded his Guild of Handicraft in 1888; in this he was also inspired by *Mackmurdo*'s Century Guild. The Guild of Handicraft was based in Essex House, near Toynbee Hall, from 1890, and produced Arts and Crafts metalwork and furniture. In 1900 Ashbee met *Wright* in Chicago. In pursuit of the rural life, he transferred his Guild to Chipping Camden in Gloucestershire in 1902 and it survived until bankruptcy in 1908. Its products are characterised by an earnest amateurishness in their hand-hammered, attenuated metal, embellished with enamel or cabochon stones. Ashbee also practised as an architect and wrote polemical books on the social implications of craftsmanship.

BEHRENS, Peter (1869–1940)

German painter, graphic designer and architect. He was a graphic artist until 1901 when he built his own house at the Darmstadt artists' colony, two years after having been invited there by its patron, the Grand Duke Ernst Ludwig. From 1906 he established the 'corporate identity' of AEG, the vast German electrical company, producing architecture, graphics, kettles, fans and clocks for the firm. In 1907 he became a founder of the Deutscher Werkbund. At one time in 1910 *Le Corbusier*, *Gropius* and *Mies van der Rohe* all worked in his office. Behrens has been called a pioneer of Modern design, but his preservation of the traditions of the Renaissance and *Schinkel* suggest how far he was in fact a classicist.

BEL GEDDES, Norman (1893–1958)

American artist and designer. He became an

industrial designer in 1927, and his book *Horizons* of 1932 is a vision of streamlining, which became associated with him. He designed visionary cars, air liners and buses, and for a period in the early 1930s taught Eero *Saarinen*. *Horizons* had enormous influence on the design of the Chrysler Airflow Car of 1934.

BELL, John (1811–1895)
British sculptor and designer, trained at the Royal Academy from 1829. Bell was a member of Sir Henry *Cole*'s Summerly's Art Manufactures from 1847 and designed much Parian porcelain statuary for Minton, as well as bread and paper knives for the Summerly group. His best-known sculpture is probably *America*, which stands at one of the corners of the Albert Memorial in London.

BENNEY, Gerald (b.1930)
British silversmith, trained at Brighton College of Art and the Royal College of Art. He set up his London workshop in 1955 and was Consultant Designer to Viners Ltd from 1957 to 1969. He was Professor of Silversmithing and Jewellery at the Royal College of Art from 1974 to 1983.

BENSON, William Arthur Smith (1854–1924)
British architect and designer. A friend of *Morris* and Burne-Jones, Benson became from the 1880s the leading designer of Arts and Crafts metalwork, especially in brass and copper. He was a great innovator, and designed vacuum flasks and the most intelligently conceived electric lamps of the day, which were exhibited throughout Europe, especially at *Bing*'s. His furniture revives eighteenth-century forms and makes frequent use of metal fittings. Benson became director of Morris & Co. on the death of Morris in 1896, and lived on to become a founder in 1915 of the Design and Industries Association, Britain's answer to the Deutscher Werkbund.

BERTOIA, Harry (1915–1978)
Italian-born American designer. Educated at the Cranbrook Academy of Art 1937–9, he taught metalwork there from 1939 to 1943. He met both Eliel and Eero *Saarinen* and *Eames* there, and later joined Eames in California in 1943. He then worked on chair design, producing his 'Diamond' welded steel wire

chair for Knoll in 1952, and from the 1950s practised mainly as a sculptor.

BING, Samuel (1838–1905)
German businessman. Bing worked in a ceramic factory in Hamburg before the Franco-Prussian war, and in 1871 moved to Paris to open a shop. He travelled to Japan and China in 1875, a year before Dresser did the same. In 1877 he opened an oriental warehouse in Paris, befriended Louis Comfort *Tiffany*, and sold the latter's glass. His shop 'La Maison de l'Art Nouveau', established in 1895, sold glass by Emile Gallé, René Lalique and Karl *Köpping*, as well as by Tiffany. He published *Artistic Japan* between 1888 and 1891 and *Artistic America* in 1895, and, more than any one else, had his finger on the international pulse of Art Nouveau.

BRANDT, Marianne (1893–1983)
German metalworker. Studied at the Bauhaus, from 1923 to 1925 under Laszlo *Moholy-Nagy*, whose Constructivist forms inspired her greatly. Moholy turned her from an Arts and Crafts metalworker in 1924 into an industrial designer of lamps in 1925. She was head of the metal workshops at the Bauhaus from 1928 to 1929, worked for *Gropius* in 1929 and then became a freelance designer and teacher.

BRANZI, Andrea (b.1938)
Italian architect. Founded Archizoom in 1966 in Florence with *Deganello* and others, with whom he worked until 1974. In 1977 Branzi helped to organise the 'Italian Design of the Fifties' exhibition in Milan, and wrote the introduction to a book of the same title in 1979. In the same year he worked with Studio Alchymia and in the 1980s has produced furniture design for the Memphis group. His book *The Hot House*, published in 1984, is an excellent and important survey of Italian 'new wave' design.

BREUER, Marcel (1902–1981)
Hungarian-born architect and designer. Breuer worked at the Bauhaus from 1920, and from 1925 to 1928 taught there as head of the furniture workshop. His first chairs of wood imitated *Rietveld*'s De Stijl furniture, but from 1925 he began to design chairs in tubular steel, inspired by an earlier experiment by

Mart *Stam* using gas piping as well as by technology wrought from bicycles and aircraft. From 1933 Breuer designed aluminium furniture, and between 1935 and 1937, when he was a refugee in England, he worked in plywood. In 1937 he joined *Gropius* at Harvard. He was one of the most gifted Modern furniture designers of his age, and versions of his chairs are still in production.

BURGES, William (1827–1881)

British architect. Inspired by *Pugin* and thirteenth-century French architecture. He designed furniture from 1858, some painted by Burne-Jones, Rossetti and Poynter, and metalwork from the same date. He was patronised by the millionaire Marquis of Bute from 1865, and though his work is mainly in a robust Gothic revival style, he could produce hybrid forms and interior effects that anticipate Post-Modern colour and humour by a century.

CHEKHONIN, Sergei (1878–1936)

Russian ceramic designer and graphic artist. Trained at St Petersburg School of Design 1896–7. After the October Revolution of 1917 Chekhonin was appointed director of the Lomonossov porcelain factory in Petrograd (Leningrad), a position he held until 1927, when he left for Paris. He was responsible for much of the 'agit-prop' porcelain of the period, brightly painted with colourful slogans on imperialist blanks taken over when the factory was seized during the Revolution. Although he was born in the same year as *Malevich*, he was less of an innovator and created no new shapes for porcelain. He died in Germany.

CLEMENTS, Eric (b.1925)

British silversmith. He studied at Birmingham College of Art and at the Royal College of Art from 1949 to 1953. He specialised, in the 1950s, in the design of ceremonial silver, and became a consultant designer for Mappin & Webb Ltd as well as Head of the Industrial Design School at Birmingham College of Art.

CLIFF, Clarice (1899–1972)

British designer and ceramicist, trained in Burslem, Stoke-on-Trent. In 1918 she went to work for a local pottery, A.J. Wilkinson, and from about 1925 she designed Art Deco patterns, brightly coloured and aptly called 'Bizarre', at one of their branches, the Newport Pottery. She directed this pottery until 1963, and is remembered for being a British interpreter of 'jazz age' forms in suitably garish colours.

COLE, Henry (1808–1882)

British watercolourist, civil servant, reformer of the postal system, designer, author and founder of the South Kensington Museum. From 1841, using the pseudonym Felix Summerly, he published books and Christmas cards, and from 1846 he designed ceramics for Minton. His group Summerly's Art Manufactures was launched in 1847 and included *Bell* and *Redgrave*. Cole was instrumental in setting up the 1851 Great Exhibition, and with *Pugin, Jones* and Redgrave selected objects to form the basis of a design museum, first as part of the Government Schools of Design, from 1852, and from 1857 at the South Kensington Museum, which at the end of the century became the Victoria & Albert.

COPIER, Andries Dirk (b.1901)

Dutch designer. He joined the Leerdam glass factory during the First World War, and after further studies became design director in 1927. He was from the first interested in mass-produced glass which echoed the functionalism of the Modern movement, and this reached fruition in his severe forms of the 1930s. Copier left Leerdam in 1970 after over half a century, and in the 1980s began to design glass again, at Murano in Italy.

CRANE, Walter (1845–1915)

British painter, engraver and designer. He designed books from the 1860s and was influenced by Japanese art in the 1870s. In that decade he came to know *Morris* and Burne-Jones. He was already well known in Europe by the time he was made principal of the Royal College of Art in 1898. Crane absorbed Morris's Socialism and design style. His late work, which was shown by *Bing* in Paris, heralds Continental Art Nouveau, and often mixes Greek and Japanese sources. A prolific publisher and designer, Crane's books and illustrations helped to disseminate the Arts and Crafts style widely.

DAY, Robin (b.1915)
British designer, educated at the Royal College of Art from 1935 to 1939. A chair designed by Day won first prize in the Museum of Modern Art's 'International Competition for Low Cost Furniture Design' in New York (1948), where his work was noticed by Hille, who appointed him their design consultant from that date. His furniture won a gold medal at the 1951 Milan Triennale. Day's early work captured the spirit of the Forties and Fifties in plywood, but his pioneering polypropylene chair of 1963 was one of the most important British contributions to design since the Mini car. Day married Lucienne Conradi in 1942. Her textile designs of the 1950s are excellent examples of the period, and her 'Calyx' pattern of 1951 was named the best textile on the US market in 1952.

DEGANELLO, Paolo (b.1940)
Italian architect and designer. Deganello graduated from Florence University in 1966. He taught architecture in Florence, and at the Architectural Association in London between 1971 and 1972 and again in 1974. With *Branzi* he founded Archizoom in Florence in 1966, and worked with that group until 1974. Deganello's furniture of the early 1980s, especially for Cassina, belongs to the Fifties revival in its free form and asymmetry.

DE LUCCHI, Michele (b.1951)
Italian architect and designer. De Lucchi graduated from Florence University in 1975 and taught there until 1977. In that year he collaborated with *Branzi* in organising the 'Italian Design of the Fifties' exhibition in Milan. He subsequently contributed to Studio Alchymia and from 1979 worked with *Sottsass* as a design consultant for Olivetti. Since 1981, again with

Sottsass, he has worked for Memphis and also designed shops for Fiorucci. He is one of the most prolific and promising of the 'new wave' Italian designers.

DE MORGAN, William (1839–1917)
British painter, ceramicist and tile-maker. In the 1860s he designed glass for *Morris*, and from 1869 pottery. He succeeded where Morris had failed in producing hand-crafted tiles, inspired by Hispano-Moresque lustreware and 'Isnik' colours, and became the leading tile designer of the age. His pottery was at Chelsea between 1872 and 1881; in the following year he moved closer to Morris's Merton Abbey works, but in 1888 returned to London. This last, Fulham factory failed in 1907 and De Morgan became a writer, an occupation he shared with many Arts and Crafts intellectuals in their declining years.

DE PAS, Jonathan (b.1930s)
Italian architect and designer. De Pas formed a design team with Donato D'Urbino and Paolo Lomazzi in their native Milan in 1966, the same year as the foundation of Archizoom. They used modern techniques such as pneumatic housing structures and contributed widely to Italian Pop design. Their recent work, however, especially their furniture for Zanotta, has become relatively sober.

DRESSER, Christopher (1834–1904)
British botanist and designer. Dresser studied at the Government Schools of Design from 1847 to 1853, and from 1854 lectured there on botany. He wrote two books on this subject and received a doctorate from Jena University in 1860. He was elected a Fellow of the Linnaean Society in 1861, but turned to design in about 1862 after the publication of his *The Art of Decorative Design* and after seeing Japanese objects at the London 1862 Exhibition. Dresser designed for most of the major British carpet and textile manufacturers. He travelled to America, Japan and China in 1876–7, and collected Japanese goods for Tiffany & Co. in New York. In 1879 he established an oriental warehouse in London, and began to design ceramics on a large scale for the Linthorpe Pottery in Yorkshire. Between 1879 and 1885 he produced many designs for electroplate. He also set up the Art

Furnishers' Alliance in 1880 to sell his furniture designs and ceramics, and in that year became editor of the influential *Furniture Gazette*. His book *Japan, its Architecture, Art and Art Manufactures* was published in 1882. In the 1890s he ran a studio which mainly produced designs for textiles. He died on a business trip to Mulhouse. Dresser was an innovator of functional good-form metalwork, but his eclectic ceramics exhibit his mastery of ornament and humour.

DREYFUSS, Henry (1904–1972)

American industrial designer. He studied at the Ethical Cultural School in his native New York, worked with Norman *Bel Geddes*, and became a stage designer. He set up his own design consultancy in New York in 1929. In the 1930s he designed trains, telephones, typewriters and tractors. Dreyfuss was concerned with ergonomics, before the name was invented, and summed up his aims in the title of his book of 1955, *Designing for People*. He was a member of the American Society of Industrial Designers from its foundation in 1944, and in 1965 became its president.

DU PASQUIER, Nathalie (b.1957)

French artist and designer of textiles. Self-taught, she travelled in Africa, India and Australia from 1975 to 1978. She returned to her native Bordeaux for a year to study drawing and in 1979 went to Rome and finally Milan. She has designed fabrics for Studio Rainbow since 1980, and for Memphis since 1981. She also produced work for Fiorucci in 1982.

EAMES, Charles (1907–1978)

American architect. Studied architecture at Washington University, St Louis, and taught at the Cranbrook Academy from 1936. Worked with Eero *Saarinen* from 1939 and in 1940 they won first prize for a moulded plywood chair at the 'Organic Design in Home Furnishings' competition organised by MOMA in New York. Eames married Ray Kaiser in 1941, and moved to California to work on plywood, producing furniture and splints for the Navy. He was joined there by another Cranbrook colleague, *Bertoia*, in 1943. Eames's plywood furniture was a great success at his exhibition at MOMA in 1946. In 1948 he became interested in newer materials and produced a fibreglass chair. His laminated rosewood and leather lounge chair and ottoman of 1956, which resembles an aircraft seat, has become a classic. His own house at Pacific Palisades, California (1949) was a prefabricated steel-frame building and was much admired by designers.

FINLAY, Ian Hamilton (b.1925)

British poet and artist. Finlay went briefly to Glasgow School of Art before war service. After the war, he wrote and worked as an agricultural labourer before establishing his Wild Hawthorn Press in 1961. Here words and images were used together in cards and pamphlets. His most resolved art work is the entirety of his house, Stonypath, now called Little Sparta, at Dunsyre in Lanarkshire. It would be incorrect to fit him into any camp, but Post-Modernists have seen him as part of the classical revival.

FULLER, Richard Buckminster (1895–1983)

American architect. Studied at Harvard between 1913 and 1915, and after war service in the Navy and various posts, he developed his 'dymaxion' principle, based on the Modern movement's idea of getting more out of less. Fuller designed his Dymaxion House in 1927 and his Dymaxion Car in 1933, a year after founding the Dymaxion Corporation in Connecticut. He developed his famous geodesic domes from 1947, and they were used, for example, on the United States Pavilion at Expo 67 in Montreal.

FURNESS, Frank (1839–1912)

American architect. Furness trained in his native Philadelphia in 1857, and worked for Richard Morris

Hunt in New York before going to fight in the Civil War. From 1866 he practised with the Anglophile architect George W. Hewitt, and through the latter was inspired by British botanical ornament, especially that of *Jones* and *Dresser*. His Pennsylvania Academy of Art, completed in time for the Philadelphia 1876 Exhibition, contains metalwork influenced by Dresser, though he was also indebted to French architecture. *Sullivan* studied under Furness in 1873 before moving to Chicago, and always remembered his interest in ornament.

GAUDÍ I CORNET, Antonio (1852–1926)

Catalonian architect. Gaudí studied architecture at Barcelona University from 1873 to 1878, absorbing the Gothic revival tradition. He designed cast-iron lamps in 1879, and was always interested in metalwork: his father had been a smith. He evolved his artistic version of Art Nouveau in Barcelona, at the Casa Vicens of 1883–5 and the Güell park and palace completed in 1890. The sculptural, unfinished cathedral of La Sagrada Familia represents his most visionary project, but the architecture and furniture of the Casa Batlló of 1904–5 are most typical of his use of bony, asymmetrical forms. Gaudí pressed broken tiles and pots into service in some of his buildings, thereby displaying a love for the *objet trouvé* long before painters did the same. His work still exerts enormous influence over architects in Barcelona today, and is almost universally admired for its wit, colour, humour and inventiveness.

GIBSON, John (1790–1866)

British sculptor. Apprenticed to cabinet-makers in Liverpool in 1804, Gibson later worked for sculptors. He submitted a work to the Royal Academy in 1816 and travelled to Italy in 1817, remaining there until 1844. He returned to England to make a polychrome statue commissioned by Queen Victoria. Gibson had introduced polychromy into sculpture in 1839, and his *Tinted Venus*, begun in 1850 and shown at the International Exhibition of 1862, was the most famous experiment in that direction. Indeed, it was still famous enough to fetch £1800 in 1890 and £600 in 1916, at a time when the taste for Victorian sculpture was declining.

GODWIN, Edward William (1833–1886)

British architect. He trained in his native Bristol under its city engineer, William Armstrong, before setting up his own practice there in 1853. The town halls he designed for Northampton in 1861 and Congleton in 1864 were robust interpretations of Ruskinian Gothic. He was a pioneering collector of Japanese artefacts from 1862; after his move to London in 1865 he assisted his friend William *Burges*, who also admired Gothic and Japanese design. Godwin's artistic interests were very wide-ranging: as his son, Edward Gordon Craig, wrote, he 'was already well known as a theatre critic . . . his ideas about furniture and modern dress were discussed by all those who were interested in the new aesthetic movement'. Godwin designed furniture in various styles from 1867, but his best-known work is the simple Anglo-Japanese 'Art Furniture' produced by William Watt. From 1874 to 1878 he collaborated with his friend the painter James Abbott McNeill Whistler. Oscar Wilde referred to Godwin as 'one of the most artistic spirits in England', and one of Godwin's last commissions was the decoration of Wilde's house in Tite Street, in 1884.

GRAVES, Michael (b.1934)

American architect. After leaving the Graduate School of Design at Harvard University in 1959, Graves taught architecture at Princeton University from 1962. He was a member of the 'New York Five' group of architects in the early 1970s and was known largely for his drawings until the completion of his Post-Modern Public Services Building, Portland, Oregon, in 1982. The furniture he designed for Memphis in the early 1980s and for Sunar, as well as his metalwork for Alessi, has made him better known in the sphere of Post-Modern design.

GRAY, Eileen (1878–1976)

Irish designer, trained at the Slade School of Art from 1898 and in Paris from 1902, where she specialised in oriental lacquer. In 1922 she opened a gallery there. Gray was inspired by De Stijl and the International Modern movement, and her tubular steel furniture of the 1920s often transcends the boundary between Art Deco 'Moderne' and International Modern. Her furniture was admired by *Le Corbusier*.

GRETSCH, Hermann (1895–1950)

German designer. Gretsch studied engineering in his native Stuttgart, and wrote a doctoral thesis and two books on eighteenth-century German ceramics. He was an important member of the Deutscher Werkbund, and in 1931 designed the classic functionalist '1382' tea-set for Arzberg Porcelain. He also designed metalwork for C. Hugo Pott and, on Wilhelm *Wagenfeld*'s invitation, glass for the Vereinigte Lausitzer glassworks. The '1382' set won a medal at the Milan Triennale in 1936 and was produced throughout the Nazi period: a version exists made for the use of the SS and stamped with its initials.

GROPIUS, Walter (1883–1969)

German architect. After studying architecture between 1903 and 1907, he worked for *Behrens* from 1908 to 1910. His earliest pre-First World War furniture was neo-classical. He was a member of the Deutscher Werkbund and in 1919 succeeded *Van de Velde* as head of the Weimer School of Arts and Crafts. This became the Bauhaus, first at Weimar and then in 1925 at Dessau, in a new International Modern building designed by Gropius himself. Gropius otherwise designed very little, but as director of the school was a major influence through his selection of staff, for example *Moholy-Nagy*. He went into private practice in 1928, having appointed Hannes Meyer as Bauhaus director. After a period in England between 1934 and 1937, during which he designed some furniture for *Pritchard*'s Isokon group, he emigrated to America to become Professor of Architecture at Harvard. In 1945 he founded the Architects' Collaborative (TAC), which produced, amongst other things, architecture and ceramics for Rosenthal.

GUIMARD, Hector (1867–1942)

French architect. He graduated from the Ecole des Beaux-Arts in 1885, and in the 1890s developed his characteristic Art Nouveau style, exemplified by the Castel Béranger in Paris of 1894–8 and his sinuous work for the Paris Métro from 1900, especially the ironwork station entrances. He also designed porcelain for Sèvres, and bronze vases. Guimard is always associated with Parisian Art Nouveau, and by 1914 his career was effectively over. He emigrated to America in 1938, and died in New York. Art Nouveau was sometimes called *style Guimard* or even *style bouche de Métro* as a result of his influence.

HILL, Oliver (1887–1968)

British architect and designer. Hill was encouraged by *Lutyens* and from 1910 had his own practice. His furniture and architecture of the 1920s and 1930s embraced eighteenth-century revivalism, 'Vogue' Regency and a version of Modern which included the use of chromed steel. In the late 1930s International Modern and Art Deco 'Moderne' tended to predominate in his work. Hill designed the British Industrial Art Exhibition held at Dorland Hall in 1933.

HOFFMANN, Josef (1870–1956)

Austrian architect and designer. He studied under Otto Wagner, who recommended him for the post of Professor of Architecture at the School of Applied Arts in Vienna in 1899. In 1903, backed by Fritz Wärndorfer, Hoffmann and *Moser* founded the Wiener Werkstätte, partly inspired by *Ashbee*'s Guild of Handicraft. Hoffmann's best building is the Palais Stoclet, Brussels, of 1911. His work for the Werkstätte had a square emphasis derived from *Mackintosh*, and also included neo-classical forms with fluting and, in the 1920s, neo-rococo and 'decadent' forms. He was one of the most eclectic and versatile designers of this century.

HOLLEIN, Hans (b. 1934)

Austrian architect. Studied at the Vienna Academy of

Graphic Arts until 1956; then at the Illinois Institute of Technology, Chicago, until 1959 and the University of California until 1960. He travelled and worked in architectural offices in Australia, South America, Germany and Sweden before setting up his own office in Vienna in 1964. Hollein's work includes the Retti candle shop, Vienna (1965) and the Schullin jewellery shop in the same city (1974). Perhaps the most gifted of all Post-Modernist architects and designers, he has produced work for Memphis in 1981 and Alessi in 1983, and furniture for Poltronova. He has taught at the Art Academy at Düsseldorf since 1967, and since 1976 at the Vienna College of Applied Arts. His recent architecture includes the museum at Mönchengladbach (1981). Hollein has also written on Otto Wagner, in 1978.

HORTA, Victor (1861–1947)
Belgian architect and designer. He studied architecture and drawing at the Ghent Academy from 1874 to 1877, and from 1881 was at the Brussels Academy. His Tassel house in Brussels, completed in 1893, was a fully resolved demonstration of Art Nouveau, and was followed by his house for Armand Solvay of 1895.

ISSIGONIS, Alec (b. 1906)
British car designer, born in Turkey. He came to Britain in 1921, and studied engineering at Battersea Technical College until 1928. From 1933 to 1936 he was a draughtsman with Rootes Motors Ltd, before joining Morris Motors, with whom he stayed until the company became British Leyland. His most important designs include the Morris Minor of 1948, the Mini of 1959, and the Morris 1100 of 1962. His most famous car, the Mini, has been in production for nearly thirty years, and is approaching the Volkswagen as a design classic in terms of longevity and importance.

JACOBSEN, Arne (1902–1971)
Danish architect. Jacobsen trained at the Royal Danish Academy of Fine Arts from 1924 to 1927. His free-form chairs of the 1950s, beginning with a moulded plywood chair of 1952 for Fritz Hansen, are characteristic of that decade: his 'Egg' and 'Swan' chairs were produced for the Scandinavian Airlines hotel in Copenhagen in 1958. His designs in stainless steel, especially for Stelton, have been very successful and his 'Cylinda' line for them won the Danish Industrial Design prize in 1967. Jacobsen also designed furniture for his St Catherine's College, Oxford, in 1963.

JENCKS, Charles (b. 1939)
American writer. Graduated from Harvard in English literature in 1961 and in architecture in 1965, and received a doctorate in architectural history from London University in 1970. He has written brilliantly on Modern and Post-Modern architecture: his books include *Modern Movements in Architecture* (1973), *The Language of Post-Modern Architecture* (1977) and *Post-Modern Classicism* (1980). In addition to writing and lecturing, Jencks has designed his own 'symbolic furniture' for the 'Thematic House' in London, created in association with the Terry Farrell Partnership in 1983, and silver for the Alessi tea and coffee set competition in 1983.

JENSEN, Georg (1866–1935)
Danish silversmith. He studied sculpture at the Royal Danish Academy of Fine Arts from 1887 to 1892. From 1900 he worked as a silversmith and jeweller, and opened a workshop in Copenhagen in 1904. His early work was a robust blend of Art Nouveau and British Arts and Crafts metalwork. He encouraged the painter Johan Rohde to collaborate with him from 1907, and the latter evolved a simpler style for Jensen's firm in the 1920s, by which time it was becoming a household name for good modern Scandinavian design.

JENSEN, Søren Georg (1917–1982)
Danish silversmith. Like his father, Georg *Jensen*, he studied sculpture at the Royal Danish Academy of Fine Arts, in 1945, after serving his apprenticeship in the family firm in 1936. He was head of the Jensen design section from 1962 to 1974, when he went back to sculpture. His work won a gold medal at the Milan Triennale in 1960.

JOHNSON, Philip (b.1906)
American architect. Graduated from Harvard in 1930, and was director of the Department of Architecture and Design at the Museum of Modern Art, New York, in 1930–36 and 1946–54. He was joint author with H.R. Hitchcock of *The International Style* in 1932 and did much to further the International Modern movement. Johnson worked on the 1934 'Machine Art' exhibition, and in 1947 wrote on *Mies van der Rohe*, with whom he worked on the Seagram building. Johnson later began to rebel against International Modern architecture, and his 'Chippendale' A.T. & T. building in New York, conceived in the mid-1970s and finished in 1984, has been seen as a volte-face from Modern to Post-Modern architecture.

JONES, Owen (1807–1874)
British architect and designer. He studied at the Royal Academy from 1829, and in 1832–4 travelled to Egypt, Greece, Turkey and Spain. Jones became interested in polychromy in architecture, and between 1836 and 1845 published his *Plans, Details and Sections of the Alhambra*. He went on to produce many chromolithographic books, culminating in the *Grammar of Ornament* of 1856. He was responsible for the decoration of the interior of the 1851 Exhibition in primary colours, and in 1858–9 repeated this experiment in iron and glass buildings, notably his showroom for Oslers, the glass manufacturers. His works had enormous influence, both on his great English follower *Dresser* and in America, where his pupil Jacob Wrey Mould introduced polychromy in architecture to New York in 1855 and Frank Lloyd *Wright* studied the *Grammar of Ornament*.

KNOX, Archibald (1864–1933)
Manx designer. Knox studied at Douglas School of Art in the Isle of Man from 1878 to 1884, and went on to teach there. He moved to London in 1897, where he was helped by *Dresser*, and from 1898 began to design for *Liberty*. Knox's work forms part of the fashionable 1890s Celtic revival, and he designed silver and pewter for Liberty using interlace decoration and enamel from 1899. He also designed textiles and gravestones, including that of Liberty himself in 1917. His work was sold by Liberty's until the 1930s but he gave up designing for them before the First World War and travelled and taught in England, America and the Isle of Man. His designs, especially in silver, are among the most refined examples of British metalwork of the Edwardian era.

KOPPEL, Henning (1918–1981)
Danish silversmith, trained (like Georg and Søren *Jensen*) as a sculptor at the Royal Danish Academy of Fine Arts in Copenhagen in 1936–7 and in Paris in 1938 under the sculptor Malfrey. He spent the war in Sweden and returned to Copenhagen in 1945. From that date he worked for the Georg Jensen firm, designing free-form jewellery and silver in the 1950s. His work won him gold medals at the Milan Triennales in 1951–7. He also designed ceramics for Bing & Grøndahl from 1961 and glass for Orrefors from 1971.

KÖPPING, Karl (1848–1914)
German glass-designer and etcher. Köpping began his career by studying chemistry. His first work in Berlin was reproductive engraving, but he turned to etching in 1890 and became a professor at the Berlin Academy in 1891. At the end of the 1890s Köpping began to produce fragile iridescent flower-form glass, blown by candle and with the characteristic thinness of Art Nouveau. Many of his pieces were made by Friedrich Zitzmann at Wiesbaden. From 1896 Köpping was an editor of the Art Nouveau magazine *Pan*,

where his etchings of nudes, as well as of his own glass, were reproduced.

KUHN, Beate (b. 1927)
German sculptress and ceramic artist. Kuhn studied art history at Freiburg University in 1947–9, before working at Wiesbaden and Darmstadt. She was a freelance designer for Rosenthal between 1953 and 1962, and has had her own studio-workshop in Buedingen-Duedelsheim since 1957. Her free-form ceramics are characteristic of the Fifties decade.

LE CORBUSIER (1887–1965)
Swiss architect. Le Corbusier travelled in Italy and Austria and worked in Auguste Perret's office in France before going to Germany in 1910. There he worked in *Behrens*'s office before further travels. In 1917 he settled in Paris, where he met the painter Amédée Ozenfant with whom he developed 'Purism' from Cubism. Le Corbusier became fascinated by Greek architecture and by machinery, and in 1923 published his important book *Vers une architecture*. The International Modern emphasis in his work was revealed in his *L'esprit nouveau* pavilion at the 1925 Paris Exhibition and his white concrete houses of the period. In the late 1920s he designed tubular steel furniture in association with Charlotte Perriand and these luxurious pieces have become classics of Modern design. For the rest of his career he concentrated on architecture and planning; his work of the 1950s made a conscious break with the formalism of his earlier style and turned towards greater freedom of expression.

LIBERTY, Arthur Lasenby (1843–1917)
British entrepreneur. In 1862 Liberty became manager of the oriental warehouse in Regent Street established by Farmer & Rogers in the wake of the growing interest in Japanese goods. The firm closed in 1874, and Liberty set up his own business in the same street in the following year. He visited Japan in 1888–9, and in 1910 wrote a book based on his visit. He commissioned fabrics and furniture which made his firm famous to this day and even gave the name *stile Liberty* to Italian Art Nouveau. The firm worked in association with *Dresser* in the 1890s, and commissioned silver (known as 'Cymric') from 1899, and pewter (known as 'Tudric') from 1901 from Archibald *Knox* and Reginald Silver. The firm ceased to produce this metalwork at the end of the 1920s when it became involved in the Tudor revival.

LINDSTRAND, Vicke (b. 1904)
Swedish glass designer. Studied at the Swedish School of Arts and Crafts, Göteborg, in 1924–7. From 1928 he was a designer with the Orrefors glassworks in Sweden, leaving in 1941 to set up the Ekebybruk ceramics factory. In 1950 he became a director of design at the Kosta glassworks, where he remained until 1973. He is well known for his free-form glass and glass engraving.

LISSITZKY, El (1890–1941)
Russian artist. He studied architecture in Darmstadt in 1909–14, and in 1915–16 was at Riga Polytechnic, at that time evacuated to Moscow. Between 1917 and 1919 he was involved with Jewish culture and books, and in 1919 was asked by Marc Chagall to teach graphics and architecture at Vitebsk. Lissitzky was influenced by *Malevich*, joined the latter's UNOVIS group and developed Suprematism into his own PROUN (Project for the Affirmation of the New); this was 'a half-way station between architecture and painting'. In 1921 he went to Moscow to teach at the Vhkutemas, the official design college of the Soviet Union. In the 1920s he travelled frequently, establishing contact with Dada artists, the Bauhaus in Germany and De Stijl in Holland; in 1924 he met *Stam* in Switzerland. He returned to the Vhkutemas in 1925 to teach interior and furniture design in the metalwork and wood faculty. In 1930 he designed an armchair that is clearly based on Bauhaus experiments. Like *Moholy-Nagy*, Lissitzky was always experimenting with design, photography, photograms, graphics, typography and book design; his last work in 1941 was a propaganda poster, 'Provide More Tanks'.

LOEWY, Raymond (1893–1986)

French designer; naturalised American. Loewy trained in France as an engineer and moved to New York after serving in the First World War. He was a graphic and theatre designer until 1929, when he streamlined a Gestetner duplicating machine. He set up his design office in the following year, and redesigned the 'Coldspot' refrigerator for Sears Roebuck in 1934, Greyhound buses in 1935 and streamlined locomotives for the Pennsylvania Railroad in 1937, as well as Electrolux appliances in 1939. Loewy became one of the best-known international designers, with offices in New York, Paris and London, and went on to produce objects for the NASA space programme until 1972. He was so prolific that in the 1950s an estimated 75 per cent of Americans came into contact with one or more of his designs every day.

Loos, Adolf (1870–1933)

Austrian architect. He studied at the Dresden Institute of Technology and travelled to America between 1893 and 1896, and from 1897 wrote on design and architecture. He admired English clothes and American plumbing, and loathed ornament, especially that of the contemporary Wiener Werkstätte. This loathing culminated in his famous article of 1908, 'Ornament and Crime'. His own architecture was inspired by neo-classicism and *Schinkel*, and his visionary Doric column, entered for the 1922 Chicago Tribune competition, continues to inspire Post-Modern architects. Apart from buildings he designed very little, preferring eighteenth-century furniture and detesting Art Nouveau. His simple water pitcher and glasses, however, originally designed in 1931 for the Loos Bar in Vienna, are still being manufactured by Lobmeyr in Austria.

LUTYENS, Edwin (1869–1944)

British architect. He entered the Kensington School of Art in 1885, but did not complete the course. In 1887 he trained with the architect Ernest George, and in 1889 he received his first commission and set up on his own account. His style embraced Arts and Crafts, Queen Anne and neo-classicism. He was the architect of the Cenotaph in London and the vast complex of imperial architecture at New Delhi, India, as well as

of many English country houses. Lutyens was an idiosyncratic and humorous designer, totally impervious to the European International Modern movement. Until quite recently, he was one of the most unfairly neglected figures of the twentieth century.

MACKINTOSH, Charles Rennie (1868–1928)

British architect and designer. Mackintosh studied at the Glasgow School of Art from 1885. In 1889 he joined the architects Honeyman and Keppie, where he became an excellent draughtsman and befriended H.J. MacNair. Mackintosh and MacNair worked with the Macdonald sisters, Frances and Margaret, in the 1890s, designing posters and metalwork. Their work was published in the *Studio*, and in 1897 Mackintosh won the competition for the design of the new Glasgow School of Art building and was also asked to design tea-rooms for the formidable Miss Cranston in Glasgow. He became known in Europe, especially in Vienna, where he designed the Scottish section for the 1900 Vienna Secession exhibition. Mackintosh's designs embrace the Arts and Crafts, Pre-Raphaelitism and the Celtic revival, and are seminal for Art Nouveau, but he was little appreciated in England. His only real work there was for the toy-train magnate W. J. Bassett-Lowke in Northampton, for whom he designed adventurously, using plastic among other materials, in 1916–17. He then almost entirely gave up architecture for watercolour painting, and lived at Port-Vendres in the Pyrenees from 1923 to 1927. His watercolours continue the beauty and colour range of his fabric designs of the 1890s, which were unparalleled in their brilliance.

MACKMURDO, Arthur Heygate (1851–1942)

British architect and designer. Apprenticed to T. Chatfield Brooks and the Gothic revival architect James Brooks from 1869. In 1873 he attended *Ruskin*'s lectures at Oxford, and assisted him during his travels in Italy in 1874. He established his architectural office in the Strand in London, and in 1880 met *Morris* and Whistler. In 1882, with Selwyn Image and Herbert Horne, he set up the Century Guild. They designed furniture, textiles and books, which were exhibited with success from 1884 to 1887. Some of Mackmurdo's furniture pays tribute to fashionable Queen Anne styles, whereas his patterning extends Morris's rhythms to the point where it could be called proto-Art Nouveau. This can be seen, for example, in his designs for the Guild's magazine, *The Hobby Horse*, started in 1884. The idea of the Guild inspired C. R. *Ashbee*, while rectilinear elements within Mackmurdo's furniture were a strong influence on *Voysey*. The Century Guild was wound up in 1888, and about 1904 Mackmurdo ceased to practise, devoting his career to issues of social and currency reform.

MALEVICH, Kasimir (1878–1935)

Russian artist. Studied at Kiev Drawing School, 1895–6, and Moscow School of Art, 1904–5. He was inspired in turn by Impressionism, Cubism and Futurism, as well as by icons. In Petrograd (Leningrad) in 1915 he developed Suprematism, a form of abstract art comprising geometric shapes against a white ground; he described these works as 'the Supremacy of pure emotion'. After the Revolution, he taught in Moscow, and then from 1919 at Vitebsk. In 1920 he founded the UNOVIS group, which included El *Lissitzky* and *Suetin*. In 1922 he returned to teach in Petrograd. He became interested in architecture and design from 1919, and in 1923 designed important ceramics inspired by Suprematism for production at Lomonossov, where his follower Suetin worked. In 1927 Malevich visited the Bauhaus, and wrote a book, *The Non-Objective World*, which was published by the Bauhaus as part of a series on Modern design.

MEIER, Richard (b.1934)

American architect. Educated at Cornell University, and employed in various architectural practices from 1957 to 1963, including Skidmore Owings and Merrill and Marcel *Breuer* and Associates. He established his own office in 1963, a year after taking up a teaching post as Professor of Architectural Design, Cooper Union, New York. Meier's architecture, for example his house at Old Westburg, Long Island, New York (1971), comes close to the spirit of *Le Corbusier* in the 1920s. He has designed a *Malevich*-inspired silver set for Alessi (1983) and *Hoffmann*esque metalwork for Swid Powell. His work is neo-Modern, not Post-Modern, and is a fascinating extension of the work of the 'heroic' inter-war period of Modern design.

MELLOR, David (b.1930)

British silversmith and designer. Educated at Sheffield College of Art, 1946–8, and at the Royal College of Art until 1953. He set up his workshop in his native Sheffield, centre of the British cutlery industry, in 1954. His 'Pride' cutlery won an early Design Centre award in 1957, and he has been well known for flatware ever since. Mellor set up his own factory, again in Sheffield, in 1974, and shops in London from 1969. He has been a consultant to Walker & Hall, British Rail and the Department of the Environment, for whom he designed traffic signals between 1965 and 1970. Mellor was chairman of the Design Council Committee of Inquiry into standards of design in consumer goods in Britain between 1982 and 1984, and served as chairman of the Crafts Council in the same years. He was made a Trustee of the Victoria & Albert Museum in 1984.

MENDINI, Alessandro (b.1931)

Italian designer. He worked with Nizzoli Associates in his native Milan until 1970. From 1970 to 1976 he edited the architectural magazine *Casabella*, and in 1979 took over the editorship of *Domus*. Mendini propagated the concept of 'banal' design in collaboration with Studio Alchymia, his most famous pieces being the redesign in 1978 of a 1940s sideboard with decoration inspired by Kandinsky, and his 'Proust' armchair painted in divisionist technique, also in 1978. His 'The Banal Object' exhibition at the 1980 Venice Biennale brought this interest in anti-design to the fore. He designed silverware for Alessi's 1983 competition and has collaborated with the firm in developing its product image. In 1983 he was appointed lecturer in design at the Vienna Design School.

MIES VAN DER ROHE, Ludwig (1886–1969)

German architect. Trained as a stonemason in his family's business between 1900 and 1902; from 1905 he was apprenticed to the architect Bruno Paul in Berlin, and to Peter *Behrens* in the same city from 1908 to 1911. From then until war service he was in private practice in Berlin, and again after 1919. His earliest work was inspired by *Schinkel*, but between 1919 and 1921 he was, like *Gropius*, interested in Expressionism in architecture. He then became involved in the International Modern movement, becoming Vice-President of the Deutscher Werkbund from 1926 to 1932 and Director of the Werkbund Weissenhof-siedlung exhibition in Stuttgart in 1927. From that date Mies designed simple, functional cantilevered tubular steel chairs; his interest in Modern but luxurious architecture and furniture found full expression in the pavilion he designed for the Barcelona Exhibition of 1929. He was appointed Director of the Bauhaus in 1930, having refused the post in 1928. He moved the school from Dessau to Berlin but failed to save it; it closed in 1933. He stayed in Nazi Germany until 1938, when he became Professor of Architecture at the Illinois Institute of Technology in Chicago, a post he held until 1959. Mies made high-rise slab blocks acceptable in the United States, especially in Chicago. From the 1940s his furniture was produced by Knoll, and much is still being made. In 1985 attempts to bring a posthumous building designed by Mies to the Mansion House site in London finally failed, and the alternative plans by James Stirling for the site indicate the conservationist and Post-Modernist tendencies of the mid-1980s.

MOHOLY-NAGY, Laszlo (1895–1946)
Hungarian-born artist, writer and photographer. Moholy studied law at Budapest University until he was called up in 1914, returning to the subject after the war. During the war he began to draw, and in 1919 he went from Hungary to Vienna, and then in 1920 to Berlin. He became interested in both Dadaism and Constructivism, and produced work for the avant-garde Hungarian magazine *MA* and for Herewath Walden's progressive 'Der Sturm' gallery. *Gropius* invited him to join the Bauhaus early in 1923. Moholy-Nagy reformed the metalwork studios, where his teaching influenced *Wagenfeld* and *Brandt*. He practised book design and typography, made films, took photographs and taught at the Bauhaus until 1928, when he left for Berlin, where he designed for the theatre. He moved on to Holland in 1934, and

in 1935 settled in London. Gropius, who was also in England, recommended his appointment as director of the New Bauhaus in Chicago in 1937. The school failed, and Moholy-Nagy set up the independent School of Design in Chicago; it was renamed the Institute of Design in 1944 and was directed by him until his death in 1946. His books were among the most significant contributions to design and art education at this time. They include *The New Vision, from Material to Architecture* of 1928, and *Vision in Motion*, published posthumously in 1947. His greatness is summed up in the obituary notice by Paul Citröen, who was one of his pupils: 'Moholy burst into the Bauhaus circle, ferreting out . . . the still unsolved, still tradition-bound problems in order to attack them . . . There never lived anyone more devoted to an objective cause.'

MORRIS, William (1834–1896)
British artist, designer, writer and entrepreneur. Morris went to Exeter College, Oxford, in 1853 to study divinity. There he met Edward Burne-Jones; both read *Ruskin* and turned towards careers in art and architecture. Morris articled himself in 1856 to the Oxford office of the Gothic revival architect G.E. Street, where he met Philip *Webb*. He moved with Street's office to London, where he shared a house with Burne-Jones. In 1857 he began to paint, under the guidance of Dante Gabriel Rossetti; together they were involved in the painting of frescoes at the Oxford Union debating hall. Webb built his Red House at Bexleyheath in 1859, and the difficulty of finding suitable decorative work for the house prompted him to set up Morris, Marshall, Faulkner & Co. in 1861, with Ford Madox Brown, Burne-Jones, Webb and Rossetti as colleagues. He began to design wallpapers in 1862, the first examples being produced in 1864 and the bulk dating from the 1870s. He began to lecture in 1877, and in the same year founded the Society for the Protection of Ancient Buildings, as well as beginning to weave and to make carpets in Hammersmith. In 1881 he moved to Merton Abbey to set up looms; here he was close to his friend the Arts and Crafts tile-maker *De Morgan*. Morris's last Arts and Crafts gesture was to set up the Kelmscott Press, which produced beautiful hand-made books between 1891 and

1898. One of the first was Ruskin's *The Nature of Gothic* (1892). The Press also printed Morris's visionary poetry, and his works on Utopianism and Socialism, for example *A Dream of John Ball*, designed with Burne-Jones's assistance. Morris had embraced Socialism early in his career, but finally joined the Democratic Federation in 1883. His Socialism directly influenced *Crane* and *Ashbee*, and his reform of the decorative arts inspired Guilds and groups all over England, America, Belgium and Germany.

MOSER, Koloman (1868–1918)

Austrian designer. Moser studied painting and design at the Vienna Academy and School of Applied Arts from 1888 to 1894. He was involved in the Vienna Secession from 1897, and became a teacher at the School of Applied Arts in 1899 and a professor from 1900. He was a prolific designer of graphics, glass and ceramics and taught many students to work in the Secession style. In 1903 he founded the Wiener Werkstätte with his friend *Hoffmann* and their financial backer Fritz Wärndorfer. He also joined the Austrian equivalent of the Deutscher Werkbund. His students included the ceramics designer Jutta Sika.

MÜLLER, Albin (1871–1943)

German architect and designer. Müller studied at the Schools of Arts and Crafts in Mainz and Dresden, and taught at the School of Arts and Crafts in Magdeburg from 1900 to 1906. From 1906 he worked at the Darmstadt artists' colony, where his prolific decorative designs were influenced by *Behrens* and *Olbrich*. He was a professor at the Technical School in Darmstadt, and produced some buildings for the colony; by 1920 his architecture had embraced a decorative form of Expressionism, for example his vision for a community centre, which was published in *Alte und Neue Stadtbaukunst* in that year.

MURRAY, Keith (1892–1981)

New Zealand-born architect and designer. After war service Murray trained to become an architect at London's Architectural Association, from 1915 to 1918. He became interested in glass, especially after seeing Modern work at the Paris 1925 Exhibition and Swedish glass in 1930. He designed Modern glass for

Stevens & Williams in Staffordshire, and machine-form ceramics for Wedgwood from 1933. He also designed silver in a severe functionalist style for Mappin & Webb from 1934. His work was widely exhibited, and much praised in the mid-1930s by writers such as Herbert Read. He ceased to design in 1938, when he was commissioned to build the new Wedgwood factory, and after the Second World War he concentrated on architecture.

NOGUCHI, Isamu (b. 1904)

American sculptor and designer. Noguchi was educated in Japan and returned to America in 1918. He studied at Columbia University between 1921 and 1924; then assisted the Director of the Leonardo da Vinci Art School in New York. He decided to become a sculptor and from 1927 to 1929 went with a Guggenheim Foundation Fellowship to work under Brancusi in Paris. After a visit to Japan and China in 1930–31 he returned to America to work on the Federal Arts Project. He began to design his famous furniture and lamps in the 1940s.

NOYES, Eliot (1910–1977)

American architect and industrial designer. Born in Boston, he studied architecture at Harvard from 1928 to 1935, and again from 1937 to 1938, before working in the newly founded office of Walter *Gropius* and Marcel *Breuer* in Cambridge, Mass., in 1939–40. Gropius sponsored his appointment as Director of the Department of Industrial Design at the Museum of Modern Art, New York, a post he held from 1940 to 1942 and again from 1945 to 1946. In 1946 he assisted Norman *Bel Geddes* before setting up his own design practice in Connecticut in 1947. Noyes developed the 'corporate identity' of IBM from 1956, Westinghouse from 1960, Mobil Oil from 1964, and Pan American from 1969. He was President of the International Design Conference from 1965 to 1970.

OLBRICH, Joseph Maria (1867–1908)

Austrian architect. Studied at the State School of Applied Arts, Vienna, from 1882 and at the Academy of Fine Arts from 1890. He obtained the Rome Prize in 1893 and from 1894 worked for Otto Wagner and befriended *Hoffmann*. In 1897–8 he designed the Vienna Secession building, and in 1899 he went to Darmstadt, where he was responsible for much Art Nouveau architecture and decoration at the Mathildenhöhe complex which housed the artists' colony.

OUD, Jacobus Johannes Pieter (1890–1963)

Dutch architect. Studied at the School of Arts and Crafts in Amsterdam and the Technical University in Delft. He worked for Theodor Fischer in Munich in 1911 and in 1915 met Van Doesburg and *Rietveld*. His architecture shares the De Stijl emphasis on cubic forms. He was present at the opening of the Bauhaus exhibition at Weimar in 1923.

PAOLOZZI, Eduardo (b.1924)

British sculptor and ceramic artist. Paolozzi attended classes at Edinburgh College of Art in 1943, and after demobilisation in 1944 he went to the Slade School of Fine Arts. At this time he became interested in comics and American magazines. Between 1947 and 1950 he worked in Paris, returning to London to teach in the textile department of the Central School of Arts and Crafts until 1955. He was a member of the Independent Group at the Institute of Contemporary Arts in London, and from 1955 to 1958 taught sculpture at St Martin's School of Art. He participated in the 1956 Whitechapel Gallery Exhibition 'This is Tomorrow', which also featured Richard Hamilton's famous collage *Just what is it that Makes Today's Homes so Dif-*

ferent, so Appealing. From 1960 to 1962 he was Visiting Professor at the Hamburg School of Fine Arts and since 1968 has been Tutor in Ceramics at the Royal College of Art, London. He visited Berlin in 1974–5 and went again to Germany in 1976 as Visting Professor of Ceramics at Cologne University. In 1981 he was appointed Professor of Sculpture at the Munich Academy of Fine Arts. Paolozzi has designed ceramics for Rosenthal and, in 1984, major mosaic decorations for the London Underground system, at Tottenham Court Road station.

PONTI, Gio (1891–1979)

Italian architect and designer. Ponti studied architecture at the Polytechnic in his native Milan between 1918 and 1921, after two years of war service. He worked in a Milan architectural office in 1921 before designing ceramics, some clearly inspired by the Wiener Werkstätte, for the Richard Ginori factory from 1923 to 1930. He also practised as an architect from the 1920s, and in 1928 became founding editor of the influential design magazine *Domus*, which he controlled until his death. Ponti was director of the Monza Biennale, which eventually became the Milan Triennale, from 1925 to 1979, and Professor at the Faculty of Architecture at Milan Polytechnic between 1936 and 1961. He was also important as an architect: his most famous post-war building is the Pirelli office tower in Milan, finished in 1956 in partnership with the engineer Pier Luigi Nervi.

PORTOGHESI, Paolo (b.1931)

Italian architect. Portoghesi graduated from university in Rome, his native city, in 1957, and established his architectural office there in 1958. From 1962 to 1966 he was Professor at the University of Rome, and resumed teaching there in 1981. A leading Post-Modernist, he has directed the architecture section of the Venice Biennale since 1979, and was appointed its chairman in 1983. He has been editor of *Controspazio* since 1969 and of *Itaca* since 1977, and his book *After Modern Architecture* (1980) is an important contribution to Post-Modernism. He designed a tea and coffee set for Alessi in 1983.

PRITCHARD, Jack (b.1899)

British designer and manufacturer. Studied engineering and economics at Cambridge, after war service in the Navy. He graduated in 1922 and worked for Michelin tyres in France and then for Venesta Plywood from 1925. In 1930 he commissioned *Le Corbusier* to design a stand for Venesta, after seeing his *L'esprit nouveau* pavilion at the 1925 Paris Exhibition. He also commissioned the Canadian-born International Modern architect Wells Coates to design the Venesta stand for the British Empire Trade Exhibition in Manchester in 1931. Coates and Pritchard formed Isokon in 1931 as a British attempt to apply 'modern functional design to houses, flats, furniture and fittings'. As a result, one of the first International Modern concrete buildings in England, known as Lawn Road Flats, was built by Coates on Pritchard's land in Hampstead in 1932. As refugees, *Gropius, Breuer*, and briefly *Moholy-Nagy* all lived at these flats and contributed designs to Isokon. Pritchard designed a few plywood pieces, but the major achievements of his venture were not only the introduction of the International Modern style to England but also the production of such 'classics' as Breuer's plywood long chair and nest of tables of 1936.

PRUTSCHER, Otto (1880–1949)
Austrian designer. Attended the School of Arts and Crafts in Vienna from 1897, and taught there from 1910. He participated in the 1900 Paris Exhibition and the 1902 Turin Exhibition, and became an important textile, metal, book and glass designer for the Wiener Werkstätte, founded in 1903. He was much influenced by the designs of *Hoffmann*.

PUGIN, Augustus Welby Northmore (1812–1852)
British architect and designer. Trained as a draughtsman by his father Augustus Charles Pugin. In 1827, aged only 15, he was asked to design silver for Rundell & Bridge and furniture for Windsor Castle. Between 1834 and 1836 he was commissioned to design the decoration for the new Houses of Parliament, published three books, *Gothic Furniture in the Style of the Fifteenth Century, Contrasts* and *Designs for Gold and Silversmiths*, and converted to Roman Catholicism. Also in 1836 he was asked to build the Gothic revival Scarisbrick Hall. Pugin was the architect of numerous churches, for example St Giles, Cheadle, of 1841–6.

From 1838 Hardman & Co. in Birmingham began to make his designs for silver; Minton in Stoke-on-Trent produced his tiles from 1840, and John Crace made his furniture, wallpaper and textiles in the late 1840s. Pugin was asked to assemble the Medieval Court at the 1851 Exhibition, and he was on the purchasing committee for objects to form part of the museum set up after the exhibition. He died, overworked and insane, soon afterwards.

PUIFORÇAT, Jean (1897–1945)
French silversmith and sculptor. Puiforçat served during the First World War, and was an athlete of some distinction. He learned silversmithing from his father, L.V. Puiforçat, whose excellent collection of eighteenth-century silver eventually passed to the Louvre. He also studied sculpture with Louis Aimé Lejeune. He set up his own workshop in 1921, and exhibited Art Deco metalwork at the Paris 1925 Exhibition and again in 1937. His friend the Art Deco silversmith Raymond Templier called him 'the creator of modern silver'. Puiforçat wrote of his own geometric, Modernist work in 1933: 'I continue to believe that the circle which explains the world in its entirety is the ideal figure, and the curve, which relates to it, is more noble than the straight line.'

RACE, Ernest (1913–1963)
British designer. He studied interior design at the Bartlett School of Architecture, University of London, from 1932 to 1935, and weaving in India between 1937 and 1939. In 1945 he started Race Furniture, at that time restricted to the use of metal from aircraft scrap. His 'BA' chair of 1945 and other recast aluminium furniture followed, proving a success at the 1946 'Britain can make it' exhibition. He submitted furniture to the Museum of Modern Art's 'Low-Cost Furniture' competition in 1948, and designed outdoor chairs for the 1951 Festival of Britain site. Made of light bent steel and aptly named 'Springbok' and 'Antelope', they can be seen in many

Festival photographs, notably outside the Regatta restaurant. The bent plywood seat of 'Antelope' owes much to work by Marcel *Breuer* and Charles *Eames* in this material. Race continued as director of Race Furniture until 1954; from then on until his death he worked as a freelance designer.

RAMS, Dieter (b.1932)
German designer. Studied architecture and design at Wiesbaden School of Art from 1947 to 1948, and again from 1951 to 1953. He worked with the Frankfurt architect Otto Apel between 1953 and 1955, and has designed extensively for Braun AG in Frankfurt since that date. He was appointed Professor at the Hochschüle für Bildende Künste in Hamburg in 1981.

REDGRAVE, Richard (1804–1888)
British artist and designer. Redgrave was apprenticed as a draughtsman to his father's engineering company. He studied at the Royal Academy Schools from 1826, and from 1830 taught drawing and practised as a painter, often dealing with themes of social realism. He taught at the Government Schools of Design from 1847, and in the same year was asked by *Cole* to design for Summerly's Art Manufactures, for whom he produced ceramics, glass and papier-mâché. Redgrave was scathing about excess ornament in his supplementary report on design written after the 1851 Exhibition. He continued to teach at the Government schools, rising to become Director of Art in 1874 but resigning a year later. He was a competent designer, a good painter and an excellent theorist, and influenced *Dresser* among others.

RIEMERSCHMID, Richard (1868–1957)
German architect. Riemerschmid studied painting at Munich. In 1896 he designed his own house at Pasing, and was an early convert to the Arts and Crafts movement in Germany. With *Behrens* he founded the Vereinigte Werkstätten für Kunst im Handwerk in 1898, and in 1900 designed a room for a lover of art at the Paris Exhibition. He taught from 1902 to 1905 at the art school in Nuremberg, and in 1907 was a co-founder of the Deutscher Werkbund. He was chairman of the Werkbund between 1920 and 1926, as well as Director of the Kunstgewerbeschule in Munich between 1912 and 1924 and Director of the Cologne Werkschule from 1926 to 1931. Riemerschmid embraced classicism in his architecture, and his designs ran the gamut from Arts and Crafts furniture to Art Nouveau ceramics and machine-made artefacts of proto-Bauhaus simplicity.

RIETVELD, Gerrit (1888–1964)
Dutch furniture designer and architect. Rietveld was apprenticed from 1899 to 1906 in his father's cabinet-making shop in Utrecht, and opened his own furniture-making business there in 1911. By 1917 he was in touch with the De Stijl group, largely through contact with Robert van t'Hoff. He remained a member of De Stijl until 1931. His famous 'Red-Blue' chair of 1918 is a three-dimensional exploration of Mondrian's use of colour in painting. In 1920 he designed a Cubist-inspired hanging lamp. He was influenced by the architecture of *Wright* as well as the Modern movement. The house he built for his friend the interior designer Truus Schröder in 1924 epitomises De Stijl ideas and forms. Rietveld's furniture inspired Marcel *Breuer* at the Bauhaus, and the 'Red-Blue' chair is the most reproduced image of twentieth-century furniture design. His furniture is still being produced by Cassina in Italy, and the influence of his colour can be felt, for example, in the work of the Memphis group and other recent Italian products.

ROSSI, Aldo (b.1931)
Italian architect. Rossi studied at the Milan Polytechnic, graduating in 1959. He worked for the magazine *Casabella* until 1964, and was Professor at Milan Polytechnic from 1969 to 1972. After a period in Zurich, he returned to that professorship in 1974. He has also taught at Venice University since 1976. His architecture includes the Teatro del Mondo for the 1980 Venice Biennale, a floating theatre of wood and steel whose form also provided the inspiration for his 1983 tea and coffee set for Alessi. In 1983 he became director of the Venice Biennale architecture section.

RUHLMANN, Jacques Emile (1879–1933)
French furniture designer and maker. Ruhlmann exhibited his furniture at the Salon d'Automne from

1910. After the First World War he founded his own firm to manufacture his designs. His furniture was often inspired by eighteenth-century precedents, but used rich woods such as mahogany, amboyna and macassar ebony, often inlaid with ivory. His blending of eighteenth-century luxury with Paris modernism exemplified the Art Deco style and attracted much attention at the 1925 Paris Exhibition. Ruhlmann was commissioned to decorate the tea-room of the luxury liner *Ile de France* in 1927, and also the Government 'Chambre de Commerce' in 1930. In his last years he even used chromium-plated metal in combination with luxurious furniture for the palace of the Maharajah of Indore.

RUSKIN, John (1819–1900)

British writer and critic. Ruskin was educated privately and at Christ Church, Oxford, from 1837 to 1842. In 1843 he published the first volume of his *Modern Painters*, completed in 1860. He became interested in architecture, and the Gothic style in particular, publishing *The Seven Lamps of Architecture* in 1849 and *The Stones of Venice* in 1851–3. He wrote prolifically, and inspired *Morris* and the Arts and Crafts movement to turn away from industry for aesthetic and social reasons. He disliked railway trains, glass and iron, machine ornament and any decoration which lacked truth to materials, and wrote, for example, about the 'fatal newness' of veneered rosewood furniture. *The Stones of Venice* contains a chapter 'on the Nature of Gothic' in which the beauty of medieval craftsmanship and architecture is equated with the joy experienced in its creation. Ruskin met Morris in 1857; *Mackmurdo* studied under him at Oxford in 1873 when Ruskin was Slade Professor of Fine Art (1870–79). He held that post again from 1882 to 1884, and although increasingly arbitrary in his judgements, and sometimes even insane, he influenced the whole of the second half of the nineteenth century. His influence was also felt in America, where Charles Eliot Norton was a friend of his, and 'Ruskinian Gothic' architecture began to be produced as early as 1863.

SAARINEN, Eero (1910–1961)

American architect, born in Finland, son of Eliel *Saarinen*. He emigrated to America with his parents in 1923, and designed furniture for his father's Kingswood School for Girls in 1929 before going to Paris to study sculpture at the Académie de la Grande Chaumière in 1930–31. Between 1931 and 1934 he studied architecture at Yale; he travelled in Europe from 1934 to 1936, returning to teach at Cranbrook, and in 1937 became a partner in his father's practice. In 1940 he and *Eames* won prizes in the Museum of Modern Art's 'Organic Furniture' competition. Saarinen's post-war work included his famous fibreglass-reinforced plastic 'Womb' chair of 1946 and his 'Tulip' chair of 1957 with plastic seat and aluminium pedestal base. His free-flow architecture of the 1950s culminated in his work at the TWA Terminal building in New York, begun in 1956 and completed in 1962, which suggests the concept of flight through expressionistic upswept curves of concrete.

SAARINEN, Eliel (1873–1950)

American architect born in Finland. Saarinen studied painting at Helsinki University, and then architecture at Helsinki Polytechnic between 1893 and 1896. In 1896 he set up in practice and designed the Finnish Pavilion at the 1900 Paris Exhibition. He also designed the Helsinki railway station between 1905 and 1914, inspired by the architecture of *Olbrich*, whom he met in Darmstadt in 1907. In the same year he met *Behrens* in Düsseldorf. Saarinen's second prize in the 1922 Chicago Tribune Tower competition brought him to America in 1923, where he taught at the University of Michigan Architecture School at Ann Arbor from 1925, becoming its President from 1932 until his death. He is best remembered for his work at the Cranbrook Academy of Art, an arts and educational development sponsored by George Booth and his wife Ellen, owners of the *Detroit News*, at Bloomfield Hills, Michigan. Saarinen designed the whole complex, beginning with the Cranbrook School for Boys between 1926 and 1930 and completing it with the Museum and Library of 1943. At Cranbrook, his wife, the weaver and sculptress Loja Gesellius, designed rugs and textiles, while in 1929 their son, Eero *Saarinen*, designed furniture for the Kingswood School for Girls, which was also part of the Cranbrook enterprise. The Swedish sculptor Carl Milles worked at Cranbrook, and the school's reputation attracted *Eames*, who taught there from 1936, and *Bertoia* from 1937.

SABATTINI, Lino (b.1925)

Italian silversmith and designer. Sabattini worked in a brassware shop, and educated himself in Como during the war by reading *Domus*. He was briefly apprenticed to Rolando Hettner, a German refugee ceramicist. He moved to Milan in 1955, where he met *Ponti*, who encouraged him in his work. In the 1950s his metalwork, notably his 'Como' service for the French silver plate firm Christofle, was inspired by free-flow forms. He set up his own works at Bregnano, near Como, in 1954.

SAPPER, Richard (b.1932)

German-born designer. Sapper studied at university in his native Munich between 1952 and 1956, and designed for Mercedes-Benz until 1957. In 1958 he went to Milan, where he worked for *Ponti* until 1959 and with Marco Zanuso until 1975. Sapper and Zanuso were responsible for some of the best product design of the 1970s. Sapper's plastic and aluminium 'Tizio' table lamp of 1972 for Artemide was characteristic of the slick Seventies; his 'Bollitore' kettle of 1983 for Alessi is, however, the result of a fertile combination of Post-Modernism and the inherited high-tech of the 1970s. He returned to Germany to start his own studio in 1970, but continues to be strongly associated with Italian design.

SARPANEVA, Timo (b.1926)

Finnish designer. Trained at the Central School of Industrial Design, Helsinki, between 1941 and 1948. In 1950 he became a designer with the Iittala Glassworks in Finland, winning prizes at all the Milan Triennales from 1954 to 1960. He established his own office in 1962, and from 1970 began to design for Rosenthal. He has also designed textiles.

SCHINKEL, Karl Friedrich (1781–1841)

Prussian architect, painter and designer. Schinkel was a student in Berlin from 1794, and was inspired in 1797 by Friedrich Gilly's project to build a monument to Frederick the Great. In 1798 he attached himself to the Gilly household to study architecture. Schinkel was inspired by the neo-classical and Gothic styles, and attended the new Berlin Bauakademie from 1789. He travelled to Prague, Vienna, Trieste, Venice and Rome in 1803 and 1804, finishing his grand tour in Paris after visiting Naples and Sicily. On his return to Prussia he worked as a painter and theatre designer, but from 1810 began to practise as an architect of official Prussian buildings. In 1815 he became Under-Director of the Prussian Works Deparment, and in 1830 Director. Schinkel's buildings in Berlin are mostly neo-classical, but he admired Gothic and designed in both styles. He also studied and made drawings of British architecture and cast-iron work and visited England and Scotland in 1826. He initiated a Prussian and Germanic tradition which has, in turn, inspired *Semper, Loos, Behrens, Mies van der Rohe* and Post-Modern Classicism of the 1980s, including the recent work of James Stirling.

SEMPER, Gottfried (1803–1879)

German architect. Semper studied law and mathematics at Göttingen University from 1823 to 1825 and architecture in Munich in 1826. He then worked in France under Franz Christian Gau and Jacques Ignace Hittorf. From 1830 to 1833 he travelled in France, Italy and Greece, and with the help of *Schinkel* became director of the school of building at the Royal Academy in Dresden. Here he designed the opera house, completed in 1841. He took part in the revolution of 1849 in Dresden, and had to flee to Paris. In 1850 he went to London, where he met Prince Albert, *Cole* and the Summerly Group, and was asked to contribute to the design of some sections of the 1851 Exhibition. He taught metalwork, among other subjects, at the Government Schools of Design from 1852; *Dresser* was an admiring student. Semper became Professor at Zurich Polytechnic in 1855, where he planned the Wagner National Theatre for Bayreuth in 1864 (Richard Wagner had been a friend at the time of the 1849 revolution). Between 1869 and

1876 he worked on important museum architecture in Vienna. He was much influenced in the 1830s by Hittorf's interest in polychromy, and one of his earliest publications was a pamphlet on the use of colour in architecture (1834). His essays and books, 'Die Vier Elemente der Baukunst' of 1851, *Wissenschaft, Industrie und Kunst* of 1850, and *Der Stil* of 1861–3 attempt to classify and order architecture and the decorative arts in a scientific manner. His own stylistic preferences, expressed in his practical work, were neoclassical and Renaissance; it is perhaps significant that he retired to Italy and died in Rome.

SOTTSASS, Ettore (b.1917)

Italian architect and designer. Sottsass studied architecture at Turin Polytechnic from 1935 to 1939, and after war service opened his own office in Milan in 1946. He became design consultant to Olivetti from 1958 and set up a design studio for the company at Ivrea, near Turin, in 1960. He designed the 'Elea' computer for Olivetti in 1959, as well as the 'Praxis' and 'Valentine' typewriters in 1963 and 1969. Besides producing such examples of 'good form', Sottsass became a father-figure of 'anti-design' in the 1960s. He produced furniture based on Pop Art for Poltronova from 1966, and Indian-inspired ceramics in 1969. The anti-design aspect of his work increased after 1979 when he became associated with Studio Alchymia, and in 1981 he formed the Memphis group, which continues this tradition. Of late, Sottsass's Memphis designs – for example his 'Hyatt' table of 1984 – even pay homage to Post-Modern Classical work by *Hollein*. The ambiguity of Sottsass's approach to design makes him a key figure in Post-Modernism, in that he is able to reject 'good form' where necessary for the sake of light relief.

STAM, Mart (1899–1986)

Dutch architect. Studied to be a draughtsman in Amsterdam and Rotterdam until 1922, when he moved to Berlin. Here he met El *Lissitzky*, worked on a Bauhaus exhibition, and designed one of the earliest cantilevered tubular steel chairs in 1925. He worked on flat-roof International Modern housing for the Weissenhofsiedlung in Stuttgart in 1927, and was asked to teach at the Bauhaus in 1928–9. He was a socially committed architect, and he worked in the Soviet Union with the architect Ernst May between 1930 and 1934.

SUETIN, Nikolai (1897–1954)

Russian artist and designer. Suetin served in the First World War between 1915 and 1917, and from 1918 to 1922 went to Vitebsk Art School. He joined *Malevich*'s UNOVIS group in 1919, and when Malevich left Vitebsk for Petrograd (Leningrad) in 1922, Suetin followed him. He worked with Malevich on Suprematist architecture, and from 1923 was employed at the Lomonossov state porcelain factory in Petrograd. His Suprematist designs and shapes are among the best products of Soviet porcelain. By 1930 his style had returned to a stylised folk realism. Suetin became the artistic director of Lomonossov in 1932, and worked there until 1952. One of his students was Eva *Zeisel*.

SULLIVAN, Louis Henry (1856–1924)

American architect. Sullivan studied architecture at Massachusetts Institute of Technology in 1872–3 and then left his native Boston to work in Frank *Furness*'s office in Philadelphia. The crash of 1873 sent Sullivan to Chicago to seek employment with the architect William Le Baron Jenney; then in 1874–5 he studied at the Paris Ecole des Beaux-Arts. He became chief draughtsman in the Chicago office of Dankmar Adler in 1881; by 1883 they were full partners. Frank Lloyd *Wright* worked for them between 1888 and 1893. Sullivan inherited an interest in ornament from Furness and the Beaux-Arts tradition, and passed it on to Wright. His high-rise office buildings in Chicago and New York, such as the Guaranty Building, Buffalo, New York (1891–6) are excellent expressions of American architecture. Although he was a master of ornament, he wrote in his essay 'Ornament in Architecture' (1892) that 'it would be greatly for our aesthetic good if we should refrain from the use of ornament for a period of years', and in 1896 he made his famous statement 'Form ever follows function. This is the law'. Sullivan's writings were worshipped by Wright until the very end of the latter's career.

TATLIN, Vladimir (1885–1953)

Russian artist. Studied at the Moscow Art School, 1902–4, Penza Art School, 1904–9, and again at Moscow, 1909–10. From 1908 he associated with the painters Mikhail Larionov and Natalya Goncharova; he was a Cubo-Futurist painter and sculptor until the Revolution, when he commenced his monument to the Third International, the model for which was exhibited in 1920 in Moscow and Petrograd (Leningrad). In 1919 he moved to Petrograd, where he set up a quasi-architectural studio to study 'volume, material and construction'. There he attempted to reform design, especially of clothes and ovens, in 1923–4. From 1925 to 1927 he was in Kiev, where he began to teach the 'culture of materials'. In 1927 he returned to Moscow to teach at the Vkhutein, in both the wood and metalwork and the ceramics faculties. In association with N. N. Rogozhin he designed a bent-wood chair with a moulded seat in 1927, and milk jugs of hand-sculptural inspiration in 1930. Both appear to be attempts at a design language similar to that of the Bauhaus. In the 1930s he worked on a project for a glider – the Letatlin – and returned to painting, which towards the end of his life became figurative.

TEAGUE, Walter Dorwin (1883–1960)

American industrial designer. Studied at the Art Students League in New York from 1903 to 1907. Teague did a variety of design jobs before setting up one of the first design consultancies in New York in 1926. He worked for Kodak from 1928 until his death, and also designed car bodies, coaches and service stations as well as products for Corning Glass, Steuben Glass and Pyrex. He was founder and first president of the American Society of Industrial Designers, which was formed in 1944 and numbered *Dreyfuss* and *Loewy* among its members.

THUN, Matteo (b. 1952)

Austrian-born designer. Thun studied sculpture at the Oskar Kokoschka Academy in Salzburg before taking a degree in architecture at Florence University in 1975, where he designed a flying machine. He was a founder member of the Memphis group in 1981, lives in Milan and has been a prolific designer of ceramics. Since 1982 he has taught ceramics and product design at the Vienna Academy of Arts, and has worked with *Sottsass* as a member of Sottsass Associati.

TIFFANY, Louis Comfort (1848–1933)

American artist and designer. Son of Charles Louis Tiffany (1812–1902) who founded the New York silversmiths in 1834; Tiffany senior began manufacturing jewellery in 1848, absorbing Edward C. Moore's silver firm in 1868. L.C. Tiffany studied painting with George Innes and Samuel Colman from 1866 to 1868, and then under Léon Bailly in Paris until 1869. He travelled to Spain, North Africa and Egypt in 1870 before returning to New York. In 1877, after the Philadelphia 1876 Exhibition, he founded the Society of American Artists with Innes, Coleman and John La Farge, from which, in 1878, he formed Louis C. Tiffany and Associated Artists. This led to many commissions, including the red and blue rooms in the White House in Washington of 1882–3. Tiffany was encouraged in his orientalism by Edward C. Moore, and began designing stained glass at Thills Glass House, Brooklyn, from 1876; in 1880 he began making 'art glass' at the Heidt Glass House, Brooklyn, with the help of a Venetian glass-blower, and patented his iridescent 'Favrile' technique. In 1895 *Bing* asked Tiffany to make ten stained-glass windows for his shop in Paris, 'La Maison de l'Art Nouveau'. These were designed by artists including Bonnard, Vuillard, Sérusier and Toulouse-Lautrec. Tiffany Studios were set up in 1900 to make bronze and lamps; Tiffany won a gold medal at the Turin 1902 Exhibition for an Art Nouveau lily cluster lamp. He became Art Director of his father's firm on the latter's death in 1902, and spent over two million dollars on his artists' colony house, Laurelton Hall at Oyster Bay, Long Island, built between 1902 and 1904. Tiffany Studios closed in 1932, a year before Tiffany's death, but Tiffany & Co. continues to be a prestigious and elegant enterprise in New York to this day, and has recently re-established a shop in London.

TUSQUETS, Oscar (b.1941)
Spanish architect. Tusquets attended the Higher Technical School of Architecture in his native Barcelona and in 1965 formed Studio PER there in partnership with the architect Lluís Clotet, with whom he worked until 1984. He has designed furniture for Casas in Spain and submitted an organic silver set to the 1983 Alessi tea and coffee service competition.

UTZON, Jørn (b.1918)
Danish architect. Utzon studied at the Academy of Fine Arts in Copenhagen from 1937 to 1942. He worked for *Aalto* in Helsinki in 1946 and for *Wright* at Taliesin in 1949. In 1956 he won first prize in the competition for the New Opera House in Sydney; however, he had to resign from the project in 1966 as a result of interference with his work, and the building was completed by others in 1973. Utzon contributed strongly to the organic style of the 1950s.

VAN DE VELDE, Henri (1863–1957)
Belgian architect and designer. He studied painting from 1881 to 1884 at the Académie des Beaux-Arts in his native Antwerp, and under Carolus Duran in Paris from 1884 to 1885. He became a Post-Impressionist and Symbolist painter, but, influenced by *Morris* and the British Arts and Crafts, he turned to design in 1892–3. In 1895 he built an organic, Art Nouveau house for himself at Uccle. *Bing* saw this, and asked Van de Velde to design rooms for his shop, 'La Maison de l'Art Nouveau', in 1895; a similar commission came from Julius Meier-Graefe to furnish his own shop, 'La Maison Moderne', in 1899. Meier-Graefe introduced Van de Velde to German designers

associated with the Art Nouveau magazine *Pan*; his work had already been seen in Dresden in 1897. He went to Germany in 1899, where he designed much, including the interior of the Folkwang Museum at Hagen between 1900 and 1902. He was an adviser to the Grand Duke of Saxe-Weimar from 1901 and designed silver for the court jewellers. In 1906 he designed the Weimar School of Arts and Crafts building and became director of the school when it was completed in 1908. He joined the Deutscher Werkbund on its foundation in 1907, but was too much of an individualist to remain there after his clash in 1914 with Hermann Muthesius over the latter's insistence on standardisation. He designed a theatre for the 1914 Werkbund Exhibition in Cologne, but the outbreak of war made him an alien in Germany. *Gropius* was appointed to take over the Weimar School of Arts and Crafts, and Van de Velde left for Switzerland in 1917. From 1921 to 1924 he was in Holland, and from 1925 until 1947 in Belgium. He retired to Switzerland in 1947.

VASARELY, Victor (b.1908)
Hungarian artist, working in France. He studied medicine, then art at the Poldini-Volkmann Academy in Budapest in 1927 and at the Mühely Academy (known as the 'Budapest Bauhaus') from 1928 to 1929. One of his teachers there was *Moholy-Nagy*. In 1930 Vasarely went to live in Paris. It was only in 1947 that he moved towards abstract Op Art. He began to produce designs for ceramic murals as early as 1954, one of which was for the University of Caracas, Venezuela. He has contributed designs for Rosenthal ceramics and tiles for the exteriors of their 'Studio Houses' in Germany.

VENINI, Paolo (1895–1959)
Italian glass artist. Venini studied law in Milan. He opened a glass factory at Murano in 1921, and another in 1925. His early style was simple and functional, and was praised at the Monza Biennale of 1923 and the Milan Triennale of 1933. He worked with *Ponti* from 1927. His firm is most famous for its 'Handkerchief Bowl' (*vaso fazzoletto*) of the 1950s, a modern form which uses traditional methods of embedding threads of white or coloured glass within a clear glass body.

VENTURI, Robert (b.1925)

American architect. He studied architecture at Princeton University from 1943 to 1950, before working under the architects Eero *Saarinen* and Louis Kahn. From 1954 to 1956 he was Rome Prize Fellow at the American Academy in Rome. He taught at the University of Pennsylvania School of Architecture from 1957 to 1965 and his work there formed the basis for his seminal book *Complexity and Contradiction in Architecture* of 1966. He then became Professor at Yale, and a graduate seminar which he taught with his future partner and wife, Denise Scott Brown, and Stephen Izenour in 1968 provided the material for his second book, *Learning from Las Vegas* (1972). Venturi opened his architectural office in 1964 in his native Philadelphia, and the firm has been known as Venturi, Rauch and Scott Brown since 1967. He is a major exponent of Post-Modernism and Post-Modern Classicism, seen for example in the split gables in the Chestnut Hill House, Pennsylvania, designed in 1962 for his mother, and in the stucco and wood house of 1982 at New Castle County, Delaware. He designed a 'Mirror in the Greek revival manner' for the 1982 Formica 'Colorcore' competition, and a silver tea and coffee service of Georgian character for Alessi in 1983. His group of nine chairs, two tables, a low table and a sofa for Knoll (1984) is his most important contribution to Post-Modern design to date. (Significantly, Knoll is better known for its International Modern furniture by *Mies van der Rohe*.) Venturi has emerged as the leader of American Post-Modern architecture and design: in 1986 he was chosen as the architect for the new National Gallery extension in London.

VOYSEY, Charles Francis Annesley (1857–1941)

British architect and designer. He was articled to J.P. Seddon and then to George Devey from 1874 until he set up on his own in 1882. He was inspired by his friend *Mackmurdo* and the precedent of *Morris* to design wallpapers, and in 1884 joined the Art Workers' Guild. In 1893 he designed wallpapers for Essex and Co. and his work was published in the *Studio* magazine. He also began to design Arts and Crafts furniture in oak, and brass metalwork for Elsley & Co. His low, vernacular, roughcast houses, for example Annesley Lodge in Hampstead (1896), are characteristic of his interpretation of the Arts and Crafts movement.

WAGENFELD, Wilhelm (b.1900)

German designer. He studied at the School of Arts and Crafts in his native Bremen from 1915 to 1918, and from 1919 to 1921 at the Hanau Drawing Academy. He then studied at the Bauhaus metalwork studios, under *Moholy-Nagy*, from 1923 to 1924, and began to work on product-design lamps. From 1926 he taught at the Bauhochschule, Weimar, where from 1929 he was in charge of the metalwork class. In 1931 he moved to Berlin, where he taught at the State Academy of Fine Art until 1935. He began to design for the Jena glassworks in 1930 and for the Vereinigte Lausitzer glassworks in 1935, remaining with the latter firm until 1948. On seeing his Jena glass in the 1930s, Moholy-Nagy admonished him for using a teardrop shape which was not sufficiently geometric. Wagenfeld produced good Bauhaus-based forms throughout the Nazi period, and served in the German army during the war. He disliked Fifties free-form 'knick-knacks', and always approached product design with great seriousness.

WARHOL, Andy (1930–1987)

American artist. He studied at the Carnegie Institute of Technology in Pittsburgh before going to New York in the 1950s to work as an advertising illustrator. He was one of America's most famous Pop artists in the 1960s. Though he announced his retirement in 1965, and was shot in 1968 by an associate, Valerie Solonas, who had formed SCUM (the Society for Cutting up Men), Warhol recovered and went on to produce neo-classically inspired images, notably the Zeitgeist paintings of 1982, such as the *Friedrich Monument*, exhibited at the Zeitgeist International Art Exhibition in Berlin in that year.

WEBB, Philip (1831–1915)

British architect. Webb trained under the Reading architect John Billing from 1849 to 1852 and then joined G. E. Street's office in Oxford as principal assistant. There he met *Morris* in 1856. He was much influenced by the writing of *Ruskin*. In 1858 he set up on his own and began to design the Red House, in Bexleyheath, for Morris. In 1861 he became a shareholder in Morris, Marshall, Faulkner and Co., and designed robust oak furniture in a stripped Gothic style. He also drew birds for stained glass and book covers, as well as designing simple table glass and metalwork based on medieval precedents.

WELCH, Robert (b. 1929)

British designer and silversmith. Trained at the Birmingham School of Art, and from 1952 to 1955 at the Royal College of Art. Welch started his own workshop in Chipping Camden in 1955, and in that year became design consultant to Old Hall Tableware. He was influenced by Scandinavian design, having visited Sweden and Norway in 1953 and 1954. Since 1960 he has been more concerned with industrial design, although he has continued to be a silversmith. He taught at the Central School of Art and Design from 1957 to 1963, and at the Royal College of Art from 1963 to 1971.

WIRKKALA, Tapio (1915–1985)

Finnish designer. Studied at Helsinki School of Industrial Arts from 1933 to 1936. In 1947 he became a designer for Iittala glass, as well as practising as a freelance. He was Art Director of the Helsinki School of Industrial Art from 1951 to 1954 and set up his own design studio in the same city in 1955. He also designed for Rosenthal from 1959 and for Venini glass from 1965.

WRIGHT, Frank Lloyd (1869–1959)

American architect and designer. As a child, he was taken to the 1876 Centennial Exhibition. He studied civil engineering from 1885 to 1887 at the University of Wisconsin, and worked for Louis *Sullivan* in Chicago from 1888 until 1893, when he opened his own office there. He had fully developed the low 'Prairie House' by 1900, for which he designed Arts and Crafts furniture, stained glass and metalwork. He designed a copper weedholder of elongated form in 1893, as well as robust, highly geometric oak chairs. In 1897 he helped to found the Chicago Arts and Crafts Society, and three years later was visited by C. R. *Ashbee*, who much admired his work. Wright himself admired Japanese and Pre-Columbian art and design,

and his Larkin office building in Buffalo, New York (1904), had metal chairs and desks which were quasi-oriental in their simplicity. He visited Europe, particularly Germany and Italy, in 1909–10, and in 1911 built his first 'Taliesin' house in Wisconsin. In 1915 he went to Japan to complete his work on the New Imperial Hotel in Tokyo. His work was admired in Europe, especially by the De Stijl group in Holland, who saw in his architecture stylistic affinities with their own ideas. He designed glass for Leerdam in Holland in 1930, but few of his designs were produced. In 1932 he founded the Taliesin Fellowship, an educational establishment for architects. His house Fallingwater, Bear Run, Pennsylvania (1936) demonstrated his mastery of the Modern style of architecture, while his Solomon R. Guggenheim Museum in New York, designed in 1943 but only completed at the time of his death in 1959, was prophetic of the 1950s style.

Z

ZANINI, Marco (b. 1954)

Italian architect. Zanini studied at Florence University until 1978, having travelled and done freelance work in California between 1975 and 1977. He joined *Sottsass* as an assistant in 1977 and has designed furniture and glass for the Memphis group in Milan since 1981. In 1980 he became a member of Sottsass Associati, the design consultancy group founded by Sottsass.

ZEISEL, Eva (b. 1906)

American ceramic designer, born in Hungary. She studied painting at the Academy of Fine Arts, Budapest, in 1925, and started her own pottery before going in 1928 to work as a ceramic designer at the Schramberg pottery in Germany. In Germany she became aware of Bauhaus and Werkbund forms, but left for the Soviet Union in 1932. There she worked at the Lomonossov porcelain factory under *Suetin*, just after his Suprematist period. She also worked for the Dulevo ceramics factory in Moscow from 1934, but left the Soviet Union in 1937 and emigrated to America in 1938 after marrying in England. She taught industrial design at the Pratt Institute in Brooklyn, New York, from 1939 to 1953. Her ceramics of the 1940s continue to observe the Museum of Modern Art principles of good form, and her style of that date is a ceramic counterpart of organic furniture. Her classic work is a service aptly named 'Museum White', designed in 1942 for Castleton China, New Castle, Pennsylvania, in collaboration with the Museum of Modern Art, New York, and produced in 1946.

SELECT BIBLIOGRAPHY

AMBASZ, E. (ed.), *The International Design Yearbook 1986/7*, London, Thames and Hudson, 1986

ARWAS, V., *Art Deco*, London, Academy Editions, 1980

ASLIN, E., *The Aesthetic Movement: Prelude to Art Nouveau*, London, Ferndale Editions, 1969

BANHAM, R., *Theory and Design in the First Machine Age*, London, Architectural Press, 1960

BATTERSBY, M., *The Decorative Twenties*, London, Studio Vista, 1976

BATTERSBY, M., *The Decorative Thirties*, London, Studio Vista, 1976

BAYLEY, S., *In Good Shape*, London, Design Council, 1979

BAYLEY, S. (ed.), *The Conran Dictionary of Design*, London, Conran Octopus, 1985

BØE, A., *From Gothic Revival to Functional Form*, Cambridge, Cambridge University Press, 1957

BRANZI, A., *The Hot-House*, London, Thames and Hudson, 1985

CAMPBELL, J., *The German Werkbund – The Politics of Reform in the Applied Arts*, Princeton, Princeton University Press, 1978

DORFLES, G. (ed.), *Kitsch: The World of Bad Taste*, London, Studio Vista, 1969

FLEMING, J. and HONOUR, H., *The Penguin Dictionary of Decorative Arts*, Harmondsworth, Penguin Books, 1979

FOSTER, H. (ed.), *Postmodern Culture*, London, Pluto Press, 1985

GARNER, P., *20th Century Furniture*, Oxford, Phaidon Press, 1980

GARNER, P., *The Contemporary Decorative Arts*, Oxford, Phaidon Press, 1980

GOMBRICH, E. H., *The Sense of Order*, Oxford, Phaidon Press, 1979

GRAY, C., *The Great Experiment: Russian Art 1863–1922*, London, Thames and Hudson, 1982

HESKETT, J., *Industrial Design*, London, Thames and Hudson, 1980

HIESINGER, K. B. and MARCUS, G. H., *Design since 1945*, London, Thames and Hudson, 1983

HILLIER, B., *Art Deco*, London, Herbert Press, 1985

HILLIER, B., *The Style of the Century 1900–1980*, London, Herbert Press, 1983

HITCHCOCK, H. R., *Architecture, Nineteenth and Twentieth Centuries*, Harmondsworth, Penguin Books, 1971

HORN, R., *Memphis*, Philadelphia, Running Press, 1985

HUGHES, G., *Modern Silver 1880–1967*, London, Studio Vista, 1967

JENCKS, C., *The Language of Post-Modern Architecture*, London, Academy Editions, 1984

JENCKS, C., *Post-Modern Classicism*, London, Academy Editions, 1980

JENSEN, R. and CONWAY, P., *Ornamentalism*, London, Allen Lane, 1982

JERVIS, S., *The Penguin Dictionary of Design and Designers*, London, Penguin Books, 1984

KRON, S. and SLESIN, S., *High Tech: The Industrial Style and Source Book for the Home*, London, Allen Lane, 1978

LODDER, C., *Russian Constructivism*, New Haven, Yale University Press, 1983

LYOTARD, J. F., *The Post-modern Condition*, Manchester, Manchester University Press, 1986

LYOTARD, J. F. (ed.), *Les Immatériaux*, catalogue of an exhibition at the Centre Georges Pompidou, Paris, March-July 1985

MACCARTHY, F., *A History of British Design 1830–1970*, London, Herbert Press, 1983

MCFADDEN, D. R. (ed.), *Scandinavian Modern Design 1880–1980*, New York, Harry N. Abrams, 1982

MADSDEN, S. T., *Sources of Art Nouveau*, London, De Capo Press, 1975

MELLY, G., *Revolt into Style*, Harmondsworth, Penguin Books, 1967

MORGAN, A. L. (ed.), *Contemporary Designers*, London, Macmillan, 1984

NAYLOR, G., *The Arts and Crafts Movement*, London, Studio Vista, 1971

NAYLOR, G., *The Bauhaus*, London, Studio Vista, 1968

OVERY, P., *De Stijl*, London, Studio Vista, 1969

PEVSNER, N., *Pioneers of Modern Design from William Morris to Walter Gropius*, Harmondsworth, Penguin Books, 1968

PEVSNER, N., *The Sources of Modern Architecture and Design*, London, Thames and Hudson, 1968

PORTOGHESI, P., *After Modern Architecture*, New York, Rizzoli, 1982

RADICE, B., *Memphis*, London, Thames and Hudson, 1985

READ, H., *Art and Industry*, London, Faber & Faber, 1934

SCHMUTZLER, R., *Art Nouveau*, London, Thames and Hudson, 1964

SCHWEIGER, W. J., *Wiener Werkstätte*, London, Thames and Hudson, 1984

SPARKE, P., *Ettore Sottsass Jnr*, London, Design Council, 1981

SPARKE, P., *An Introduction to Design and Culture in the Twentieth Century*, London, Allen & Unwin, 1986

SPARKE, P., HODGES, F., STONE, A. and COAD, E. D., *Design Source Book*, London, Macdonald & Co., 1986

STERN, R. A. M. (ed.), *The International Design Yearbook 1985/6*, London, Thames and Hudson, 1985

VENTURI, R., *Complexity and Contradiction in Architecture*, New York, Museum of Modern Art, 1966

WHITFORD, F., *Bauhaus*, London, Thames and Hudson, 1984

WINDSOR, A., *Peter Behrens, Architect and Designer*, London, Architectural Press, 1981

WOLFE, T., *From Bauhaus to our house*, London, Jonathan Cape, 1982

PHOTOGRAPHIC ACKNOWLEDGEMENTS

INDEX

Numbers in bold type refer to illustrations